Your Towns and Cities in the

# Southend-on-Sea
## in the Great War

GWEN COLLINS —FLAT 6

## Dedication

In memory of my grandfather
Private Cecil James Cutter
2nd/4th Battalion, Lincolnshire Regiment
Killed in Action, The Somme, 8 April 1917
Buried in Bray Military Cemetery

Your Towns and Cities in the Great War

# Southend-on-Sea in the Great War

Frances Clamp

Pen & Sword
**MILITARY**

First published in Great Britain in 2014 by
PEN & SWORD MILITARY
*an imprint of*
Pen and Sword Books Ltd
47 Church Street
Barnsley
South Yorkshire S70 2AS

ISBN 978 1 47382 255 9

Printed and bound in England
by CPI Group (UK) Ltd, Croydon, CR0 4YY

Typeset in Times New Roman by Chic Graphics

*Pen & Sword Books Ltd incorporates the imprints of*
Pen & Sword Archaeology, Atlas, Aviation, Battleground, Discovery,
Family History, History, Maritime, Military, Naval, Politics, Railways,
Select, Social History, Transport, True Crime, and Claymore Press,
Frontline Books, Leo Cooper, Praetorian Press, Remember When,
Seaforth Publishing and Wharncliffe.

*For a complete list of Pen and Sword titles please contact*
Pen and Sword Books Limited
47 Church Street, Barnsley, South Yorkshire, S70 2AS, England
E-mail: enquiries@pen-and-sword.co.uk
Website: www.pen-and-sword.co.uk

# Contents

| | Acknowledgements | 6 |
|---|---|---|
| 1 | Gathering Clouds | 7 |
| 2 | Fire from the Sky | 19 |
| 3 | A Year Passes | 30 |
| 4 | The Clouds Darken | 40 |
| 5 | No Peace Before Christmas | 51 |
| 6 | War at Sea | 60 |
| 7 | Death from the Skies | 69 |
| 8 | Shortages and Inflation | 79 |
| 9 | End Game | 88 |
| 10 | Aftermath | 98 |
| | Bibliography | 106 |
| | Index | 107 |

# Acknowledgements

My thanks to Nigel Cave, my extremely knowledgeable and helpful editor; The Bay Museum, Canvey Island, Alan Reed, John Rogers and all the helpers; Ken Crowe at Southend Central Museum and the staff at Southend Library; Mrs P. Porter and Westborough School and everyone at Stow Maries Aerodrome; also to Helen Finch, Mick Nash, Lois Holmes, Vic Knight, Sylvia Harrington, David and Helen Clamp, Maureen Ollett, Doreen & Bill Sawford, Heather and Fred Feather, Sylvia Kent and Susan Marriot. Above all my very special thanks to my husband Roger, without whose constant help and advice this book would have remained a dream.

# CHAPTER 1

# Gathering Clouds

The Great War of 1914-18 was unlike any previous conflict. The loss of life was on an unimaginable scale and almost everyone in the country had a relative or friend killed or injured. In this book we will specifically look at the effect of the war on the ordinary people of Southend-on-Sea. It will also be necessary to remember some of the major events both at home and abroad.

For hundreds of years Southend was simply a tiny fishing hamlet to the south of Prittlewell. However, by the middle of the eighteenth century seaside towns were becoming popular, especially as it was believed that sea air and water were good for anyone with health problems. The hamlet grew. When Princess Charlotte and her mother, Caroline, Princess of Wales, came to stay in 1801, the growing town became fashionable, although some people felt that it was too quiet to ever become really popular.

In those early years travellers often arrived by boat. This caused problems as it was only possible to drop off visitors comfortably at high tide. At other times the vast mud flats made access to the shore difficult, if not impossible. A short wooden pier was constructed. In 1834-35 this was extended and in 1846 it was lengthened once again to one and one eighth miles. Later it was completely rebuilt and extended further until it finally measured one and a third miles. The new iron pier was opened in 1889. The following year a single track electric railway started operating, the first pier railway in the country. By the early twentieth century the pier had become the symbol of the town and, although it has faced many emergencies over the years, it

*Southend pier and the Palace Hotel, known as Queen Mary's Royal Naval Hospital during the Great War.* (By kind permission of Southend-on-Sea Central Museum)

has remained one of the best known features of Southend. No one, in those early days, could have foreseen the essential part that the pier was to play in the two major conflicts of the twentieth century.

With the coming of the railway in 1856 the character of the town changed again. It could be easily reached from London. Many stayed in the large hotels that had been built to cater for their needs, but other holiday makers came for just one day. The time of the day tripper had arrived.

With the turn of the new century Southend was developing into a very popular seaside town, with a population nearing 63,000 in 1911. As 1914 dawned most people must have realised that there were growing problems in Europe, but for many who had never set foot outside the British Isles these troubles seemed to be happening in another world. However, with the assassination of Francis Ferdinand in Sarajevo awareness of the problems increased. On 5 July 1914 the Kaiser promised the support of Germany to Austria against Serbia.

Towards the end of the same month Austria declared war on Serbia. After that, events gathered speed. By the first day of August Germany had declared war on Russia and two days later on France. Belgium was also invaded. In 1894 The Treaty of London had guaranteed Belgium neutrality. With the invasion of Belgium, Britain had little choice but to declare war.

The country was celebrating bank holiday on a glorious day in summer. Like all seaside towns, this was a time for Southend traders to think of their profits, not to face the prospect of a life changing major conflict. As people returned home after the holiday they learned that Britain was at war with Germany. This was on 4 August 1914. The days of peace had ended.

Just before the outbreak of the war the 3$^{rd}$ Battle Squadron of the Home Fleet visited the Estuary and anchored off the pier. This was apparently to reassure people that there was nothing to fear from any confrontation. Our ships were powerful and ready for action. Then the Fleet sailed from Southend to Portsmouth, where it took up its battle stations. At that time the River Thames was more used to sailing boats and paddle steamers rather than the battleships that had just visited the town.

On 4 August, on hearing the news, cheering crowds hurried through the streets of London to reach Downing Street and Buckingham Palace. Many had probably been celebrating the good weather in the parks and this was a fitting end to the day. They joined in lustily with the singing of the national anthem. A feeling of patriotism filled the air. Very few believed that the conflict would last for long, many thinking that it would be over by Christmas. So, carried along by the general euphoria, large numbers of young men rushed to sign on at the recruiting offices. After all, if you did not join up early you might miss the chance. This was the gateway to travel and adventure.

According to the *Southend Standard* at the time the local reaction was very different. Apparently there was nothing of the euphoria seen in London shown by those studying the announcement in the newspaper's office window. Readers were stunned, although most must have realised that conflict with Germany was likely but it is human nature to believe that the worst will never really happen. Unfortunately now it was a reality. There was also considerable anxiety as people tried to understand why Britain was even involved.

However, momentum grew quickly. An advertisement on 15 August announced that Garons' cinema programme would include a feature called Europe in Arms. The Kursaal advertised that its building and gardens would remain open daily until 30 September. It proudly announced 'Open in Peace or War'. On 14 September another advertisement stated:

Your King and Country Need You
– A Call to Arms –

The recruiting office for the borough of Southend-on-Sea and Rochford District is at Clarence Hall, Clarence Street.
God Save the King

In the early days of the war a Sunday evening service was held in the Empire Theatre. According to the local paper, this was packed from floor to ceiling. The meeting was arranged by the borough's Anglican and Free Churches. There were prayers for peace and the singing of 'Oh God, Our Help in Ages Past'. A reading of Psalm 46 followed, as suggested by the President of the Free Church Council. This started with the words 'God is our hope and strength, a very present help in trouble'. He said this was a lesson for churches at the present time. Finally, the mayor addressed the meeting saying that, although he was in no way responsible for the gathering, he would like to tender his thanks on behalf of the town to all those who were involved.

To the east of Southend and overlooking the Thames Estuary stood Shoebury Barracks. It was to play an important role in the war. To the north was Rochford aerodrome. At one time it was just a large field where kites were flown, but it was soon adapted to make a very important contribution during the years of war.

*A soldier in full uniform ready for guard duty.* (With thanks to Bill and Doreen Sawford)

With the Thames Estuary to the south and the long pier reaching out to deep water, the town was usefully placed for the arrival and departure of shipping.  In some German reports the town was described as a fortified place and therefore a legitimate target for attacks. Not that there was too much concern that Southend might be attacked in those early days. After all, battles would be fought at the front lines in Europe. They had never been brought to civilians living quietly on home soil. Alas, all too soon, they were to learn that this war would be unlike any other.

When war was declared there were thousands of Germans living and working in Britain. It is recorded that, in 1911, there were 304 residents in Southend who had been born in Germany. Twenty-five of these were British subjects and another forty-three had been naturalised. Inevitably calls for internment grew, especially as the war progressed. Various Acts were passed to restrict the movement of those regarded as aliens. The Defence of the Realm Act of 1914 and the Aliens Restrictions Act meant that all Germans living in Britain had to register at their nearest police station. Many such citizens decided to change their names to ones that sounded English. King George V removed the Kaiser from the position of honorary colonelcy of the 1st Royal Dragoons. By 1917 even the royal family decided on a name change from Saxe-Coburg Gotha to the popularly far more acceptable Windsor.  Many regarded all aliens as a potential danger to safety and a decision was taken that those from hostile nations should be interned.  All internees were to be held as prisoners of war.

Now Southend Pier once more enters the story. It was decided to moor three prison ships off the pier, the *Ivernia,* the *Royal Edward* and the *Saxonia.* The first of these was used for German soldiers who had been captured in France. The other two ships held mainly civilians. The prisoners walked through the High Street and then along the length of the pier before boarding the ships. The tug *Memphis* was used for the purpose of transferring prisoners and supplies from the pier head to the ships. On 10 August the huge Olympia complex in Kensington was turned into a detention centre. Civilian Germans had been rounded up, many highly respected citizens, along with others suspected of being spies. Suspicion and rumour were in the air and it was a dangerous time to be 'different'. Some of these prisoners eventually came to Southend, along with others who had previously been held in York.

Even in those days councils were looking for ways to raise money. The military authorities were charged two pence for each prisoner and their escorts for the privilege of using the pier to reach the moored ships.

It may seem strange but not all prisoners were treated in the same way. On the *Royal Edward* there were three classes and it depended on how much each person could afford to pay as to the type of accommodation he received. To use the first class mess there was a charge of two shillings each day and rations were superior. You could also pay to share the comfort of a first class cabin. Those unable to afford such luxuries received ordinary rations and space in steerage, where the bunks were in tiers of three.

As we have seen Southend, with its easy access to the Thames Estuary, became a base for military personnel about to depart by ship for the continent. Large areas were needed for parades and drill and it was decided that at least one of the town's parks should be taken over immediately for this purpose. Southchurch Hall Park, later known as Southchurch Park, was selected and permission given to Colonel Patton-Bethanal, the commanding officer of the 14th Rifle Brigade, to use the park for training. However, there was one stipulation. There must be no drilling on the hallowed turf of the cricket pitch. Even in times of war it was decided that some things were too valuable to risk damaging!

Those fighting in Europe soon learnt the harsh reality of war in the twentieth century. By the end of August 1914 British troops had already fought alongside their French and Belgian allies in a bitter struggle around the town of Mons. Some 100,000 men of the British Expeditionary Force left home shores to cross the Channel. This was a highly secretive operation and the Germans had little idea that any troops had left England. The men fought bravely, but by 23 August it was realised that the situation was hopeless. A retreat began. For those fighting the early euphoria must have quickly passed.

The British suffered heavy casualties, but the conflict continued. Battles were fought along a shifting line stretching from Belgium in the north to Alsace Lorraine in the south. The main problems were in the north and in less than a month most of Belgium had been lost and

*Soldiers from the Essex Regiment relaxing.* (With thanks to Robert Welham)

the Germans had crossed the Sambre and Meuse. The French were forced to retreat to the Marne. This was the final barrier before Paris would be reached. There was defeat for the Russians too, at the battle of Tannenberg in the last days of August.

By September 1914 the war was also being fought at sea. Late in the month it was reported that three British cruisers had been sunk off the Netherlands by a German submarine. Some survivors were taken aboard another cruiser, but then it too was hit by a torpedo so the sailors were once more thrown into the sea. Mines in the North Sea also caused many deaths and casualties.

Shortly after the outbreak of war it was realised that new hospitals would be needed to deal with the many casualties arriving from France and beyond. Queen Mary agreed to give her patronage to the establishment of a naval hospital in Southend. Alfred Tolhurst was, at that time, the owner of the Palace Hotel, which towered above the sea

*Queen Mary's Royal Naval Hospital with patients on the balcony.* (By kind permission of Southend-on-Sea Central Museum)

front. He generously decided to allow the building to be used for this purpose. His offer was to be free of charge for the duration of the war. It became known as Queen Mary's Royal Naval Hospital. A number of other large hotels, buildings and halls were also taken over for hospital use.

Staffing was important in the hospitals. Women were encouraged to take courses in First Aid and general nursing. The local branch of the Red Cross became extremely important and they even took over and equipped as a hospital what had formerly been Robson Holiday Home in Southchurch Road. They were assisted by thirty ladies from the 34th Essex Voluntary Aid Detachment of the Red Cross Society. The role of women was becoming vital to the war effort and its importance would grow in the coming months and years.

Although there was only a thirty per cent increase in the number of women employed during the war, they were able to take the place of men who had enlisted. Some worked from home or in groups, such as Queen Mary's Needlework Guild and the Queen's Work for Women Fund. Often this involved knitting to provide 'comforts' for the troops. Gloves and mittens were popular and could be completed fairly quickly. Not all items were suitable and some of the military authorities felt that the well intended gifts delayed the arrival of more essential war supplies.

Factories were also places where women were able to take on useful employment. Many were involved in making munitions. For this work a special uniform was worn as there were obvious dangers involved. The Southend Corporation Electricity Works, close to the London Road, was partially converted into a munitions factory. Women were also employed in agriculture, did office work, cleaning on the railways and delivering the post. Those who worked on the land, replacing men who had gone to war, later became known as the Women's Land Army. Times were changing.

Of course men too were involved on the Home Front. They might be retired, in reserved occupations or simply unable to enlist on health grounds. Yet, for all, jobs could be found that would help with the war effort. The Southend Sewage Works became a base for the manufacture of shells, but the work there was done almost entirely by men.

By the time three weeks had passed from the outbreak of war, 250 men had volunteered to join the Special Police Force. Armed with truncheons and whistles they would be on duty in shifts, the first being from 10 pm to 2 am. The next group would take over from 2 am until 6 am and so on. These men attended all the major incidents that took place, including the early Zeppelin raids, the anti-German riots and the devastating air raid of 1917. More will be said about these happenings in later chapters.

In October 1914 a meeting was held in the Council Chamber at Southend that decided to form a Southend Battalion of the National Guard. This was known as A (Southend Company) 4th Battalion Essex Volunteer Regiment. The Company Commander was the well known proprietor of the *Southend Standard,* John William Burrows. There was a disused gravel pit in Southchurch Road and this was taken over as a temporary ground for parades and drill. Later Chalkwell Park was used for this purpose. By the end of the month 130 men had enlisted.

Far away from the Southend beaches the war in Europe was growing in intensity. Trenches had been dug and soldiers found themselves surrounded by mud and barbed wire. By mid October 1914 the problems in Belgium had increased. Ghent, Bruges and Ostend had fallen and the government had fled to France.

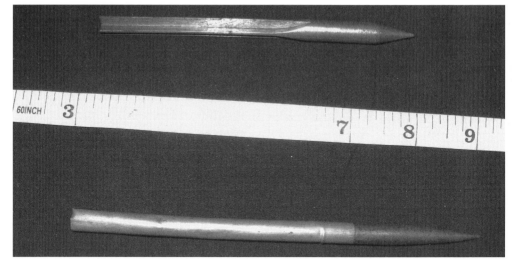

*Two flechettes. Although small when dropped from above, the heavily weighted points caused devastating damage.* (By kind permission of The Bay Museum, Canvey Island)

A new weapon had been developed by the Royal Flying Corps. Called a flechette it was a steel dart. These were heavy, sharp pointed and could be thrown in significant numbers from aircraft. When aimed accurately - not all that common or easy - at the German trenches the results could be devastating.

In late September 1914 it was reported that a great wave of Essex men had come to Shoreham for training. Included were soldiers of the 11th Battalion Essex Regiment, with many coming from the Rochford Hundred. A reporter noted that it was remarkable how little was seen of military activity in the town. In fact if it was not for the searchlights' appearing after dark people could be lulled into a belief that the war was just a dream. How things were to change in the coming months and years.

Later in the year a report came through that Major J.A. Massie of Shoebury Barracks training school had died on 13 November of wounds received in action. The obituary report stated, 'Quite a gloom was cast over the school by the intelligence. During his four year residence Major Massie had been the most popular officer there, always looking to the comfort of his men and seeing that they had all they required'.

By November trench warfare was well established. What is sometimes called the 'war of movement' had ended. Both sides had built at least three lines of trenches – a front trench, a support trench and a reserve trench. These were linked by more trenches so that men could move easily from one to another when required. However, most of those waiting at home had no idea of the conditions faced by those fighting in Europe, yet some information did get through.

Mr Heard of a local rifle club read out a letter he had received from a lady tending the wounded of the British Expeditionary Force overseas. She wrote, 'It seems ages since I left home. We've been quite in the thick of things already. Yesterday we were all sent for in a hurry to help at one of the big hospitals as a fresh lot of wounded had arrived, poor fellows. Some of the men were in an awful state. The shrapnel wounds are very awful and are in all sorts of horrible places. The men are simply wonderful. Yesterday I was nursing a poor, wounded Scottie. In his delirium he kept murmuring, "I'm nae afraid of ye Germans. Let me get a swipe in, one for Scotland and one for the bairns ye have killed".

'Another man had a bullet in his head and he swore at me when I was dressing his wound. The poor man was quite dotty and thought I was a German hurting him. I have a bullet that was taken out of the leg of another soldier. I asked him if he wanted it or whether I might keep it. He said I was welcome to it as he could soon get another when he got back to the fighting line.

'The men are all wonderfully brave. They say that if only we had more men at the front their losses would not be so bad, as they could get more rest and so be in better trim to take better care of themselves. Some are rather bitter about the slackers who stop at home and will not help their country in this hour of need, but then none of them seem to regret that they have enlisted and seem anxious to get well and back to the front.'

17 November 1914 David Lloyd George's war Budget set new rates of income tax. The new rate would be one shilling and sixpence in every pound of earned income and two shillings and sixpence on unearned income. This would hit the pockets of everyone quite severely.

As December dawned even the most optimistic citizens must have realised that the war would most certainly not end by Christmas. Then, on 16 December, not long after dawn, three German warships appeared off the east coast and started shelling  Scarborough, Whitby and Hartlepool. Over one hundred were killed, mostly civilians, and another two hundred were injured. When British destroyers went to confront the attackers, two were hit and four seamen killed. Homes were damaged and also some of the holiday hotels. The war had entered a new phase. As the people of Southend read such reports they must have wondered how long it would be before their own town came under attack from the sea.

Christmas Eve 1914 marked a new landmark in the war. This was when the first air raid on England occurred. A seaplane dropped a single bomb on Dover. As the news spread in Southend, civilians must have wondered what fresh disasters would come as the New Year dawned. Sadly they did not have too long to wait.

# CHAPTER 2

# Fire from the Sky

As the New Year dawned Southend prepared to take in even more of the wounded. The Palace Hotel, now known as Queen Mary's Royal Naval Hospital, had shown that large hotels were ideal for conversion into hospitals and recuperation centres. The Overcliff, on The Leas in Westcliff, became a Red Cross hospital in January. It was very well equipped and operating theatres were soon installed in rooms once used by relaxing holiday makers. Mr James Tabor was in charge of the committee that controlled the finances of the Overcliff and Mrs Earle became the matron. Visitors were welcomed, as they would help to raise the morale of the patients and also possibly help with fund raising. The seaside town was adapting to the war.

A new phase of warfare started on 19 January, 1915. A German Zeppelin approached the Norfolk coast in the night. Before then no one had realised the need for blackout curtains. Bombs were dropped on Great Yarmouth and King's Lynn which, according to one report, were fully lit as the airship approached from the south. Bombs were also dropped near Sandringham. It was reported that more than twenty civilians were killed and forty seriously injured. Destruction from the air was getting ever closer to Southend. War was no longer simply confined to the battlefields of Europe.

Following this attack at least one enterprising local shop decided to cash in on the need for black-out curtaining, although this was not enforced by law. Smerdons, of Hamlet Court Road, Westcliff, offered dark green or blue blinds that could be fixed without alteration to existing fittings. They could also act as sun blinds and orders could be

*Embroidered cards were often sent from troops overseas.* (With thanks to Robert Welham)

executed within a few hours. *The Daily News* offered insurance against damage from aerial attack or from the sea. Another advertisement in the local paper is interesting when realising the conditions being faced by soldiers in the trenches. Dri-ped shoe soles claimed that they were nearly as tough and enduring as Tommy himself. 'Rocky ground can't break through Dri-ped half as quickly as through ordinary leather'. Apparently the mud of Flanders could not penetrate the Dri-ped soles worn by thousands of men at the front. It also stated that Dri-ped was suitable for civilians as well as soldiers.  Life on the home front was certainly changing.

The pier was already proving useful in the war effort. The Admiralty paid for a war signal station at the pier head and later asked for it to be railed off to keep out curious members of the public. In January 1915 the Pier Master sent a letter of complaint concerning members of the 8th (Cyclist) Battalion, the Essex Regiment. He said they were riding their cycles along the pier at excessive speeds while on dispatch duty! There certainly seems to have been a conflict of interest between the civilian and military population at that point, although the pier was still used for recreation as well as being part of the war effort.

Early in February 1915 a German submarine blockade of Britain was attempted. The idea was to frighten away neutral shipping from United Kingdom waters. The British government ordered the Royal Navy to seize any cargoes of grain or flour they could capture from enemy ships. Obviously attacks on food ships would cause considerable shortages in both Britain and Germany, but by the beginning of March British naval ships were completely blockading German ports. Any ships found taking supplies to Germany would be impounded until the end of the war. This was in retaliation for German submarine attacks.

The sinking of the Cunard liner *Lusitania,* with great loss of life, led to another outburst of anti-German feeling and in Southend this was further fuelled by a Zeppelin attack on the town that resulted in the death of one woman.

The Zeppelin was a rigid airship developed by Count Ferdinand von Zeppelin. He first outlined his ideas as early as 1873 and in greater detail in 1893. The air ships were patented in Germany two years later, but were not flown commercially until 1910. Then, during the Great War, they proved to be extremely useful to the German military for both bombing and reconnaissance. The rigid, light alloy frame meant that they could be much larger than more conventional aircraft.

At first many local people simply gazed in wonder as the massive machines flew overhead, not realizing the death and devastation they could bring. All this changed on 10 May 1915. Apparently, the previous day, Sunday, had been beautiful, ideal for those enjoying a day at the seaside. Later a strong wind arose, favouring a quick passage across the North Sea. It was in the early hours of Monday morning that LZ38, commanded by Erich Linnarz, reached the town. This was the day of the first Zeppelin attack on Southend. Over one hundred bombs were dropped, although some fell in the sea and others failed to explode. The first bomb fell close to the prison ship *Royal Edward*. It missed, but the intention had probably been to hit the pier. After that the airship travelled on towards the town where a number of incendiary bombs were dropped. Apparently the shock of the noise made a horse bolt in

*The War Illustrated was a popular magazine during the war. Here we see a Zeppelin caught in searchlight beams.* (By kind permissions of the Bay Museum, Canvey Island)

*A butcher's shop in Hamlet Court Road damaged by bombing and guarded by a policeman.* (By kind permission of Southend-on-Sea Central Museum)

panic through the window of Boots the Chemist. One bomb fell in the playground of Westborough School in Macdonald Avenue, but fortunately failed to explode. The school had only been completed in 1911 and first opened its doors to pupils the following year. The building was undamaged, The Zeppelin then passed over Leigh, Canvey Island, Thundersley and Benfleet. Here it came under heavy fire from anti-aircraft guns, so it turned and headed back towards Southend. More incendiary bombs were dropped, some close to the Leigh-on-Sea Gas Works, and once more on Southend. After that it headed away towards Burnham on Crouch. In the attack four high explosive bombs fell, but only two exploded.

Some properties did suffer damage, including a butcher's shop in Hamlet Court Road, where the windows were blown in. A timber yard, belonging to Mr Flaxman, was destroyed and several houses were also damaged. The Electricity Works in London Road received some bomb damage and the local fire brigade, helped by soldiers, worked at full stretch to deal with a number of separate fires. An unexploded bomb fell in front of the Technical School at Cobweb Corner, now known as Victoria Circus. This was later removed and taken to Shoeburyness, where the military authorities dealt with its disposal. During and following the raid the firemen, soldiers and local police constables all helped to deal with the bombing and its aftermath.

Special Constable William Ledicott was on duty in Southend at the time of the attack. He described hearing the sound of the airship's propellers and then seeing the approach of the slate grey machine. For four minutes it hovered in silence over Cobweb Corner. Then the engines re-started and a bomb was dropped in the middle of the road. It made a large hole, but fortunately failed to explode. Both motor and horse drawn fire engines were used to deal with the fires caused by the bombing. Loud blasts on a hooter warned people of the attack and many rushed out of their houses, still wearing their night clothes, to see what had happened. LZ 38 managed to escape, returning later in the month to wreak more havoc.

It was later reported that Mrs Agnes Whitwell, a Southend resident, died at her home as a result of the attack and her husband was seriously injured. Newspaper reports referred to the fatality as murder. At the time of her funeral large crowds gathered to watch the procession. Afterwards anger towards Germans and Austrians grew in intensity. This was probably partly caused by the shock of the attack on home soil, something that had not been anticipated. Added to this feeling of anger was the remembrance of the earlier sinking of the *Lusitania*. Reports in the press also fuelled the feelings of hatred towards the enemy.

A special air raid supplement was published by the local paper on 15 May 1915. It showed a picture of a Zeppelin and a message that had been dropped with the bombs. It said:

You English. We have come and will come again soon.
Kill or Cure
German

Following the raid an official communiqué was issued in Berlin from army headquarters. 'One of our airships this morning dropped some bombs on the fortified place of Southend and the Estuary of the

Thames'. They certainly saw no reason to produce a lengthy supplement!

The *Southend Standard* reports were very informative, as were those in some national newspapers. In fact the Government decided that they were too detailed and contravened published guidelines. A D Notice was issued immediately afterwards, restricting the press from giving the exact location of where bombs had fallen and information concerning causalities. It was essential to keep up public morale.

In the late spring of 1915 prisoners on the ships at the end of the pier were moved away to other camps and relative safety.

The late Arthur William Hance of Wellington Avenue, Westcliff, dictated some of his memories of the Great War to his granddaughter, Karen Boyd, née Hance. He commented on the anti-aircraft guns:

> 'I have a vivid recollection of diving under the kitchen table when anti-aircraft guns first went off. They were situated where Blenhim Chase is now, just on the Leigh side of where Westcliff High School for Girls now stands. They sounded as if they were in the back garden. I can hear the "crack" even now!'

*Havens is still a popular shop in Hamlet Court Road and traded throughout the Great War.* (By kind permission of R. Havens.)

By mid May 1915 anti-German feeling intensified and there were riots in Southend. A Mr J. Harrison convened a meeting outside the Technical School at Cobweb Corner to argue for the internment of aliens. When there was a gathering of about two thousand the meeting began. The majority of those present were probably there out of curiosity, but it was later reported that others had joined to create mischief if they had the opportunity. Mr Harrison said he had arranged for speakers to come from the Port of London, but they had failed to arrive. Instead they were forced to rely on those in the crowd. Mr Warren then spoke saying that there were still a number of aliens in the town and, following the diabolical outrage earlier in the week when one woman was murdered, they should be interned. Later five shops, believed to be owned by Germans or Austrians, were attacked and wrecked.

Zeppelin LZ38 returned once more on the night of 26-27 May. Shortly after 11pm the craft passed over Shoeburyness. The garrison was ready and anti-aircraft guns were used. This caused the airship to move away towards Southend. In all seventy bombs were dropped on the town and two women were killed, one as she left a tram at Chalkwell Park. Sutton Road, Dowsett Avenue, St Helens Road, Leigh Road and Broadway Market were all hit by bombs. LZ38 once again escaped.

Many of the early patients in Queen Mary's Royal Naval Hospital were from Belgium. A report in the *Southend Standard* told of an interview with the brother of one of the wounded, Chaplain J. Holthof. He was in Southend on seven days leave from his duty with the Cyclist Corps of the 5th Division of the Belgium Army. During that time he was visiting his brother in the hospital, who was under treatment for shattered nerves, and it was there that the interview took place.

The chaplain wore The Order of the Legion of Honour of Leopold II, which had been bestowed on him by the King. The interviewer tried to discover the details of the brave action that had resulted in the award. However, the chaplain was reluctant to talk about the details and, although he spoke excellent English, seemed not to understand the question. He did say that never in all his life had he met with such kindness as he had encountered in Southend. 'I will never forget Southend and never forget the affectionate people here and their kind attention.' When the reporter tried to get him to say more about his bravery he said, 'All our men are quite as brave as I.'

*Uniform worn by nurses in the Great War.* (By kind permission of the Bay Museum, Canvey Island)

There had been some debate about uniforms being supplied to the police reserves in the town. Some women seemed to think that any man not wearing uniform must be a coward for not joining the forces. White feathers were often handed to men not in uniform, used as a symbol of cowardice. The police reserves had not been issued with uniforms and this led to some strong feelings. Letters were printed in the local press, some endorsing the suggestion of uniforms for the reservists and others opposing the idea. One thought that the officers concerned should only be issued with great coats, as they often did night duty when, even in summer, it could be extremely cold. Another contributor, arguing against uniforms, claimed that most men would prefer to wear their own clothes. In reply another stated that the writer appeared to have only taken his own opinion on the matter and it would be better to canvas the whole Force and publish the result.

In April 1915 one of the worst weapons ever to be used in modern warfare was deployed in the trenches. A group of soldiers holding the line to the north of Ypres saw a swirling greenish-yellow vapour drifting across from the German lines. Within minutes the men were coughing and, half blinded, they fled from their posts as German soldiers advanced. Gas protection at this stage consisted of wet cloths held to the faces.

As news of this development spread at home there was a sense of disbelief and then fear. After the first Zeppelin raids there was an awareness that now not only bombs but also gas could be dropped on ill prepared civilians. In late May an advertisement appeared on behalf of the Hospital and General Contracts Company. It claimed that they had developed a new respirator which satisfied all medical requirements as an initial protection against asphyxiating gasses. Apparently the respirator contained a material that, when impregnated with a special solution, neutralised the action of chlorine gases. At the same time natural breathing was possible. The eyes were protected by a transparent material that would not crack, like mica or celluloid. The mask was priced at two shillings with free postage and the special solution to be used with the respirator cost one shilling per bottle. This kit was only available from the Hospital and General Contracts Company.

There was still a desperate need for more recruits to fill the spaces left by those killed and wounded in the trenches. A letter sent home by

Private A.G.M. King of the Royal Engineers was printed in the *Southend Standard*. This paper was sent to him each week and arrived remarkably quickly. He said he had read a list of those who had recently enlisted in the town. Some were his old school friends. He then made an appeal for more to join the Forces. He believed that the war would be over by June, but if this was not the case then thousands more would be needed to fill the gaps and help to get the war finished as soon as possible. Yet there were those who were terrified that military service might soon become compulsory. On 5 July 1915 Mr Asquith assured members of Parliament that this was not the case. Not everyone believed him, especially when a National Registration Bill was passed. The government hastened to give reassurances that the registration was only for census purposes, but still many remained unconvinced.

In June Queen Mary herself visited the naval hospital.

The early months of 1915 had been bad ones for Southend with two unexpected and devastating aerial attacks. The face of war was changing and the people of the town began to realise that not just the men at the front were involved but every citizen in the country.

# CHAPTER 3

# A Year Passes

As the first year of war slowly passed there was still no sign of the conflict ending. In fact, despite efforts to calm the population, the problems in Europe grew ever greater. Positive news was published whenever possible but it did little to allay the fears of the general public.

We have already seen that a number of hotels and other large buildings in Southend had been converted into hospitals. 28 July 1915 was an important day for those who supported the hospitals and the injured military. HRH Princess Clementine of Belgium attended a gathering of supporters who had promised to bring goods to help the wounded.

A list for those wishing to assist was drawn up, stating which articles were desperately needed. Groceries and provisions, especially butter and eggs, were important, as were medical supplies. Some things may seem a little odd today but cigarettes, pipes and tobacco were all requested for the patients in 1915, along with poultry, cups and mugs, table napkins, hot water bottles, stationary and postage stamps. Slippers, pants, vests and braces were also on the list. Jam and preserves were not needed, as these had already been provided. Those donating items would not only meet the Princess but would also be given the chance to visit the hospitals involved.

There were numerous to raise money to help the war effort. George Jackerman of London Road advertised in late July that he had acquired £2000 worth of carpets bought before the war and they were being offered at much cheaper rates than was usual in 1915. Because of his

*Patients and nurses inside Queen Mary's Royal Naval Hospital.* (By kind permission of Southend-on-Sea Central Museum)

savings in the acquisition of the carpets, a five shilling War Loan voucher was being donated for every complete pound of purchases in this very special sale.

Seaside towns always rely on visitors, but as the war continued there was a new worry. Would those visitors continue to come? A conference of east coast towns took place to discuss the effect of the war on these areas. Southend's Mayor attended. Especially since the earlier Zeppelin attacks, many people had been reluctant to travel away from home and a number of local hotels were now being used as hospitals. When seasonal visitors stopped coming there were serious financial implications in the towns concerned.

It was unanimously decided at the conference to appeal to Parliament for help. The government could assure the public officially that in this time of war the east coast towns were as safe as any other coastal towns. No one need be troubled about their personal safety when visiting the resorts. It was also suggested that a series of excursions could be arranged. These would help to lighten any feelings of gloom about the state of the war. The communiqué ended by expressing the hope that the government would stand by the east coast towns, as the east coat towns had stood by the government.

At a local level the Committee of the Southend Chamber of

Commerce had been working hard to raise funds for an advertising scheme to make it clear that the town was in no particular danger from further Zeppelin raids. In fact there had been no day time raids, so those visiting should be perfectly safe. £130 had already been spent on articles in local papers in the London suburbs and elsewhere. This was in the hope that visitors would be reassured and would once more come to the town.

The cost of the war was enormous, both in human lives and also in monetary terms. September 1915 saw an increase in income tax. It rose by forty per cent and there was also a new War Profits Tax. Something that affected everyone was the rise in customs duty of fifty per cent on tea, tobacco, and a number of other goods. The Chancellor of the Exchequer, who had introduced the biggest ever Budget increase said, 'These are unprecedented burdens, but I know the tax payer is determined to see the war through.' The new rate of standard income tax was set at two shillings and eleven and a half pence in the pound.

A local man, Mr H.H. Burrows had, for several weeks, been on duty with the Red Cross close to the fighting line and he wrote to explain what was happening.

'Last week I was on special border duty and had the opportunity to hear several of our batteries open fire behind us and after an interval the German replies. Immediately we dived for a ditch and awaited results.' Apparently, following this, shells started dropping behind the Red Cross helpers. Mr Burrows continued:

> 'The shells made an infernal noise as they burst. After that they dropped to the right of us knocking about more houses and wounding several men. Then they found the road and dropped one shell right on the railway. Its rails broke just as if you took a piece of cotton and snapped it. They were left sticking up in the air. Then the range was increased a little so they fell over the road, coming more to the left.
>
> 'After we had removed one wounded man to the dressing station we decided to go back to the old spot. As pieces of shell continued to chip the branches of trees immediately in front of us we decided it would be safer to move further up the road. As I turned the enemy smacked in five shells in a hurry. We could

*An example of trench art made by Private C.R. Smith of the Essex Regiment.* (With thanks to Robert Welham)

hear them rattling about as they dropped. One piece of high explosive fell within reach of where we were sitting in the trench.'

One has to wonder what the family reaction would have been on receiving a letter like this. Obviously anyone close to the front line was in mortal danger the entire time.

Each week the names of local men who had died in action were published – a depressing list when you consider the young age of many of those casualties. One such announcement came on 2 September, 1915 when the death of Lieutenant Arthur Charles Beeton was recorded. He was the younger son of Mr C.E. Beeton, the much respected Station Master at Southend Midland Railway Station. One of the dreaded telegrams had been received by Lieutenant Beeton's parents, sent by the War Office. The young man, known to his friends as Tommy, was educated at the Southend Technical School and was later Quarter Master to the cadets there. After school he was appointed to the District Land Valuations Department at Southend and passed his examinations for the Surveyors Institute. He served for four years as a private in the London Scottish before joining the 6th Essex Regiment. The names of all the fallen from the Great War are recorded in the refectory in Priory Park.

Fortunately another story had a happier ending. Seaman Sidney Arthur Roberts belonged to the Nelson Battalion. His parents lived in Shorefields Road and were devastated to receive news that their son had been killed in action on Gallipoli on 13 July. Richard Roberts, his father, shortly after this, received two letters from other members of his division stating that his son was wounded. This confusion must have been dreadful for his family, yet all too frequently wounded men died later from their injuries. Mr Roberts decided to write to the Admiralty to try to establish the truth. This resulted in confirmation that his son had indeed died, but then he received another letter stating that his son had not been killed but had indeed been wounded on the day mentioned. A correction to the casualty list duly appeared. Although at the time of the newspaper report the family of Seaman Roberts had received no letter to say where he was being treated, but this would presumably have come later.

Those unable to serve in the forces for a variety of reasons were often able to play their part in a voluntary capacity. Members of the Southend Battalion of the National Guard were always ready to help in emergencies. When needed, they assisted the fire brigade and they were also able to help the police and military authorities in securing properties that had been damaged by bombs. This often prevented looting. Most were very proud of the fact that they were issued with uniforms and rifles. There were also specialist groups and these included the Motor Cycle and Cyclist Scouts. Among the equipment used was a motorbike with a mounted machine gun.

The Volunteer Watch was rather less formal. These men patrolled the streets in pairs, watching out for approaching Zeppelins. If any were seen or suspected of being in the area householders were warned to take shelter downstairs. Basements and cellars were especially useful. These volunteers saved police time and their work was much appreciated by ordinary citizens.

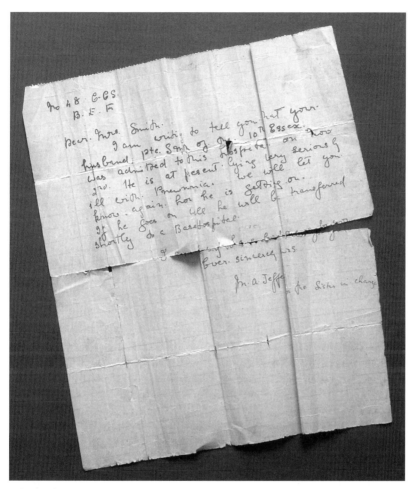

*A letter from a field hospital telling Mrs Smith that her husband, Private C.R. Smith is seriously ill.* (With thanks to Robert Welham)

At the time of the outbreak of war many boys, too young to enlist in the forces, joined the comparatively new Scouting movement. These youngsters were able to play their own part in the war effort. Shortly before the conflict started the founder of the movement, Robert Baden Powell, offered the services of his scouts to the government. Any duties they undertook were to be non military and they would be in the charge of the Chief Constable in each county. It was found that they could do useful work in a number of fields. In a seaside town like Southend they could be very helpful, especially when messages needed carrying or signals sent. All scouts learned signalling skills and they often showed great aptitude at operating wireless equipment. Early in the war they sounded bugles as air raid warnings and when the danger passed they could also sound the All Clear. The pier was an area where their presence was especially useful. They assisted in sending communications to prison ships from the pier head. Once a scout had completed twenty-eight days of voluntary service in the war effort he would be awarded a coveted War Service Badge

It was in October that it was decided in London that women could apply for licenses to be bus and tram conductors. One report said that women working in factories were twice as good as men. Some foremen, who had been very reluctant to employ women at first, commented glowingly on their punctuality and commitment to the tasks they were asked to perform. The role of women was slowly expanding and although many stopped working after the war, for others life would never be the same again. In Southend, where many women had become involved in caring for the wounded, the execution of Edith Cavell early in October must have come as a great shock. Her remains were returned to Britain after the war and a state funeral took place in Westminster Abbey. She was reburied at Norwich Cathedral in May 1919.

Lord Derby was an opponent of conscription and he was also Britain's Director of Recruitment. His brief was to boost the country's volunteer army as quickly as possible. His solution was known as the Derby Scheme. This encouraged men to voluntarily register and once they were registered they would only be called up for service when necessary. Married men were informed that they would only be required when the supply of single men was exhausted.

October saw a meeting convened by the Mayor of Southend, Alderman Joseph Francis, to consider Lord Derby's latest recruiting drive. Letters from the trenches frequently bemoaned the fact that not enough men were volunteering to join the forces and fill the gaps in the lines. A large number attended and the meeting heard details outlined. The Mayor said that he made no apology for calling the meeting because he felt that everyone would agree that the time had come for the people of Southend and the Rochford Hundred to do all

*Corporal Frederick Albert Collingwood, a descendant of Admiral Collingwood, was mentioned in dispatches, as shown by the oak leaf on the second medal, with the citation signed by Winston Churchill.* (With thanks to Mick Nash)

they could to advance the cause which all of them had so much at heart. He also said that he was delighted to see their Member of Parliament present as he had been working day and night on behalf of the great cause and they were proud to have him as their representative.

In November the *Southend Standard* reported that romance could still be found during the war. A female journalist from Leigh had visited Antwerp shortly after the start of the troubles. (Her name was not given.) There she met a Surgeon Colonel of the Belgium Army. Apparently she was instrumental in saving his life on one occasion, although no details were recorded. The friendship grew and they became engaged with the hope that, after their marriage, they would be able to settle down in Leigh. Unfortunately all their arrangements had to be put on hold as he was sent on service to Serbia.

A letter was received from Sapper D.J. Lowen of the Mediterranean Expeditionary Force telling what had happened to his brother. He had been camped on a ridge when he was hit by shrapnel. One piece struck his shoulder, but he was able to walk to the dressing station. The writer later came across his brother's haversack and, upon investigating he found only biscuits, some bully beef and a programme card for the Westcliff-on-Sea Yacht Club! The writer also described how the Turkish trenches were only twenty-five yards away. If a bomb was thrown into the allies' trenches the danger could be reduced by throwing an overcoat over it as soon as possible. After dark, as he was trying to heat a drink, a shell came over and dropped into the fire. In seconds he had grabbed his Dixie and fled to his dug-out. Whether or not the liquid was saved or was drinkable is not recorded.

Another soldier sending news to Southend said that everything was 'merry and bright' but the worst part was that they were up to their knees in mud. When it started raining it never seemed to stop.

Early December saw an announcement that many of the town's banks would be closing early in future. This was because of a shortage of staff as so many were serving in the armed forces. The notice reported that banks in Southend, Westcliff and Leigh would close at 3 pm and on Saturdays at 12.30 pm. The Banks concerned were Barclays & Company Limited, London & County Westminster Bank Limited, the Counties & Capital Bank Limited, the London and Provincial Bank Limited, the North and South Western Bank Limited and Barrows Bank. How few of those banks are still household names today.

Also in December a small party of wounded soldiers arrived in the town. Arrangements had been made for their reception by a representative from St John's Ambulance Brigade and a Dr Powers. The wounded usually seem to have been greeted in this way. As all the men could walk they were quickly transferred to motor cars provided by members of the Southend and District Automobile Club and taken to hospital.

By late December a big recruiting drive was taking place in Southend and District in answer to Lord Derby's scheme. All men under the age of forty were being asked to enlist. Apparently this was highly successful, so successful in fact that some men had to wait for six or seven hours before being medically examined. After that they were asked to attest (to take the oath.) The recruiting office in Clarence Street was obviously inadequate to deal with the rush of volunteers. The congestion became so bad that the Mayor, on learning of the situation, offered the recruiting authorities the use of the Council

Chambers for the purpose of attestation. The medical examination was dispensed with in accordance with Lord Derby's instructions. Although the recruiting drive appears to have been successful in Southend this was not the case throughout the country. Only 350,000 volunteered under the Derby Scheme and by the end of the year it was abandoned.

So the second year of the Great War drew to a close. There was no longer talk about a quick ending to hostilities. After the major recruiting drive there would be fewer men left in the town, but those remaining had to put on a brave face and look to the future with hope.

# CHAPTER 4

# The Clouds Darken

1916 did not start well. On 6 January the House of Commons voted overwhelmingly to introduce compulsory military service. The Derby Scheme was abandoned. There were two days of impassioned debate, but in the end it was decided that relying on volunteers was not enough to win the war. It was suggested that over half a million unmarried men without any health problems had failed to register under the voluntary scheme. The news of the introduction of compulsory conscription must have been very disappointing for Southend's Mayor, who had worked so hard to encourage men to accept Lord Derby's plan. The government decided to conscript only single men at first. Some ministers resigned over the decision, including the Home Secretary, Sir John Simon.

In the war zone death and severe injury continued at an alarming rate. Because of the need for ever more soldiers at the front, many of those wounded were frequently returned much earlier than would be acceptable today. One example of this was local man Lance Corporal L. Coulshaw. He was offered a commission after suffering a severe wound in Gallipoli. Although the bullet had not been extracted he was described as being well on the road to recovery. His promotion was to a battalion in the New Army and he was posted to the 12th Essex Regiment, but prior to joining that unit he was sent on a course of instruction in Oxford. Friends were asked to write to him at Keble College.

A report appeared in the *Toronto Star* of the horrific experience of another local man. Private Horace Manning, whose parents lived in

*Another example of embroidered cards often sent from the Front.* (With thanks to Robert Welham)

Leigh, was serving with the Royal Canadian Dragoons. He was in a trench with five others when a shell fell just where they were sheltering. This was a high explosive device and all six of them were blown into the air. Only Private Manning survived the blast, but he suffered concussion and severe memory loss. His nerves were shattered and he had a memory lapse about once a week which lasted for several hours at a time. At least those lapses must have given him some respite from the constant reminder of that horrifying event. Whether he was ever able to return to the Front is not recorded.

Shortages were being felt across the country, although compulsory rationing was unpopular and, where possible, avoided. In late February it was suggested by the National Organising Committee for War Savings that wealthy families should shut down part of their houses and reduce the number of servants employed. Such workers would then be available to work in more useful occupations to help the war effort. Also there was an appeal from the government that those with cars or motorcycles should stop using them for pleasure. This would, of course, hit towns like Southend that relied on holiday makers using their own and public transport. The Committee also insisted that it was a selfish and thoughtless extravagance to keep a personal chauffeur.

The *Southend Standard* regularly printed the names of men from the town and from the Rochford Hundred serving with the armed forces. A special appeal was made for residents to send in full names, local addresses, ranks and the unit to which each man was attached. It was hoped finally to publish a permanent list of all those involved.

There were constant efforts made to raise more money to help with the huge costs of the war. An advertisement for R.A. Jones & Sons, Jewellers, offered to pay exceptionally high prices for diamonds and precious stones, jewellery, old gold, silver plate, and old artificial teeth. What would happen to the latter items was not mentioned.

Letters continued to be sent home to Southend families. Private H.E. Richards, serving with the 67th Field Ambulance Forces in Salonika, wrote to say that he had been there for about three months. During that time the cold had been intense, with frost and biting winds. He had not met anyone from the town but he did gain news from the *Southend Standard*. This seems to have been sent regularly to a number of serving soldiers. He had noticed in the Casualty List that three Leigh men had been lost when the *Persia* was sunk and he sent his sympathy to the relatives. He also asked if anyone could send him a mouth organ as this would help when the men were marching. One imagines he would have received a positive response fairly quickly.

An aspect of war we may not always consider was the use of telephones by civilians during air raids. The Chief Constable complained that, during a recent raid, the transmission of urgent and important messages was interfered with on several occasions. This was because private subscribers were apparently using phones in an unnecessary and inconsiderate way. These calls were often to the police and other public officials to find out what was happening. A stern warning from the Chief Constable followed. He said that if this behaviour continued then it could become essential for the Post Master General to curtail the use of all telephones by private citizens during public emergencies.

To the east of Southend is Shoeburyness, which has a long military history. As far back as the ninth century it had been a Viking camp, although Iron Age remains have also been found and there is some evidence that the Romans built a fortified settlement in the area. It became a signal station at the time of the Napoleonic Wars. Later it was used for testing weapons and over the years it grew in size and importance. A permanent testing and practice station was established there in 1854 at the time of the Crimean War.

The beginning of the Great War saw many changes. Various units were drafted into the area and some men were billeted in the Kursaal. Troops of the Border Regiment arrived in Shoeburyness to give protection from sabotage and invasion. The garrison was also used as a transit camp for soldiers about to embark for service with the British Expeditionary Force and the trenches. For many this must have been their last time on British soil.

On 4 April 1916 King George V came to the Garrison to inspect the new ranges. Whilst there he witnessed the testing of various pieces of equipment and also inspected the School of Gunnery. It was an exciting day for local children and they lined the streets to see him pass with his entourage.

*A model of Squadron Leader Claude Alward Ridley who helped to form 61 Squadron at Rochford Aerodrome in 1917.* (By kind permission of Stow Maries Great War Aerodrome)

There was no actual attack on Shoeburyness during the war, although both Zeppelins and planes on their way to London passed overhead. Some bombs were dropped, but the damage was minimal. The only fatalities were caused during the testing of guns. Captain Lane Poole was killed in such an accident in 1915, as were five men in 1917. In that year a fire started in the ranges and as it spread the town was evacuated. This time the Kursaal once more enters the story as the evacuees were taken there to shelter until the danger was over.

After the first Zeppelin attack on Southend there was some criticism that the Garrison gave insufficient support to the town, but this was quite unfair. At that time most of the anti-aircraft guns lacked the range to trouble the airships. This situation did not last for long. Improvements were quickly made to deal with the ever increasing problems caused by Zeppelins and later from heavy aircraft raids. As the guns improved, Germany made fewer daylight attacks, relying on night time approaches instead. This meant that it was more difficult for the enemy to pin-point military targets and this probably resulted in more civilian properties being hit by random bombing.

In March it was reported locally that the fighting in Europe had recently been 'of the fiercest description'. There had been devastating losses of men on both sides and a seemingly unlimited expenditure of ammunition. All those concerned were horrified by the human sacrifice, the full extent of which had yet to be revealed to the public. Propaganda usually attempted to show only positive aspects of the war

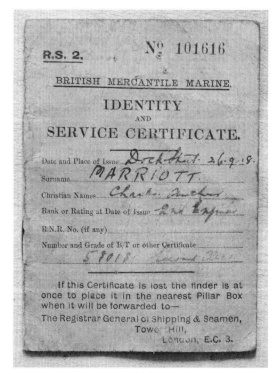

*Identity Card for Charles Marriott of the Merchant Navy.*
(With thanks to Susan Marriott Yarwood)

from the British point of view, but occasionally more detailed accounts were published.

A curious story was told concerning an officer in Egypt on a special assignment. He had been in the same unit as Lieutenant Beeston and they had been friends. Walking in an Egyptian town the officer happened to see a piece of paper on the ground that looked familiar. Picking it up he discovered that it was part of the picture page from the *Southend Standard* and there was a photograph with a caption reporting the death of his former colleague. Until that strange moment he had no idea that Lieutenant Beeston had been killed.

A big worry in Southend was the proposal to double the cost of vehicle licences. Although the number of car owners was limited this would presumably also affect coach and bus travel. Car travel was mainly reserved for the wealthy and again the holiday trade in the town would be hit.

The weather for 1916 up to April was described as wet, stormy or chilly and often all three at once. In fact some of the storms had been quite violent. People needed cheering up, but all the news, as far as the town was concerned, was exceptionally depressing. One bright point came in April with the announcement that the Government was dropping its proposed tax on rail tickets.

Various reasons were given by able bodied men claiming exemption from war service. An unusual one came from Mr A. Gilbert, boot repairer, of Hamlet Court Road, Westcliff. He was applying for his twenty-five year old assistant to be exempted, although the young man was quite willing to serve. He had previously attempted to join the Middlesex Regiment, but his employer had been unable to find a suitable replacement. The reason given for the application was that Mr Gilbert had been born deaf and dumb and he claimed that he was unable to spare the man. He had tried for at least six months to find someone else, but they lacked the necessary skills to understand sign language. His present employee had been with him for eleven years and was well able to deal with the needs of his deaf and dumb employer. The Mayor and members of the Tribunal considered this unusual application and finally decided that, although the man was more than willing to enlist, he would be granted exemption until 1 July 1916.

On 2 March, 1916 the Military Service Act came into force. This meant that, from then on, there would be conscription. The boot

*HMS Marlborough, involved in the Battle of Jutland.*

repairer might have been very willing to join up, but a fish monger from Queens Road, Southend, did all he could to avoid enlisting. The story came to light at the Southend Borough Petty Sessions. Thomas William Hills, aged 34, was charged with failing to attend at the Recruiting Office under the Military Service Act, 1916. Major Vigers, the recruiting officer, stated that the defendant had received notice to report himself on 24 March, but had failed to do so. As a result of this a notice was sent to his last known place of residence. Someone in the house, either the man himself or another acting for him, returned the notice saying that he had gone away to an unknown address. There was reason to believe that he was, at that time, resident in the house and was simply returning the notice as a scheme to avoid Military Service.

It was said that the actions of Mr Hills had put the military authorities to a great deal of trouble and expense. Although no fine was imposed on that occasion, in future cases a fine would be imposed under the Militia Act and other similar Acts. A very heavy fine would be inflicted on anyone wilfully giving wrong information in order to screen men from service. It was pointed out that it was a very serious offence to aid and abet a man who was already in default. The fishmonger was then ordered to be taken into custody to await escort, presumably to a suitable unit.

There was still a desperate need for more men to fill the many gaps in the forces. At the beginning of May plans were made to extend compulsory enlistment to married men aged between eighteen and forty-one whenever the monthly number of volunteers dropped below 50,000. Those who had previously been rejected as unfit were to be re-examined. These were desperate times throughout the country.

31 May 1916 saw the biggest naval battle of the Great War. This was the Battle of Jutland. Both sides claimed victory, but which really won is still debated. One of the ships taking part was HMS *Marlborough*. Some Southend men were almost certainly on board. Eventually the white ensign from the ship was brought to the town and proudly hung in St John's Church, close to Queen Mary's Naval Hospital. It had possibly been used to cover the coffin of a naval officer. The flag still hangs in the church today, complete with a photograph of the ship, a proud reminder of the past.

In June 1916 Lord Kitchener set off for Russia aboard the cruiser HMS *Hampshire*. Also on board was Midshipman William Richard Snowden from Southend. He had served in the Battle of Jutland without injury, but on this occasion he was far less fortunate. The ship struck a mine off the Orkneys and went down with all those on board, including Lord Kitchener. There were no survivors. William Snowden was just 19 years of age.

Southend Airport is now thriving. It even has its own railway station built close to the main terminal. Today it is hard to imagine that it had its origins in the Great War. It was the air raids that led to its establishment. It was meant to protect the area from Zeppelin attacks and those by Gotha bombers. In fact, by the time it was ready for service, many of the Zeppelin raids had ended. It first welcomed No 61 Squadron who flew Sopworth Pups, although these were later exchanged for SE5s.

When war was first declared the War Office believed that Rochford could be developed as an aerodrome for the Royal Flying Corps and at first it was used for training purposes. Then in May 1915 it was taken over by the Royal Naval Air Service. It was to be used as a night

*A RFC van.* (By kind permission of Stow Maries Great War Aerodrome)

fighter station. Later in May, A.W. Robertson left the airfield, then known as Eastwood Aerodrome, in Blériot Parasol 1546. His aim was to find Zeppelin LZ38 which had bombed Southend on 10 May and was, at that time, on its way to London. On this occasion his mission was unsuccessful. The airship was finally destroyed in June 1915. It was in its hanger in at Evere in Belgium when it was bombed by the British.

At the end of March and beginning of April 1916 massed Zeppelins attacked London. Planes from Rochford took off and gave chase, but little damage was done in Southend, or to the Zeppelins.

By June 1916 the aerodrome was once more in the hands of the Royal Flying Corps. It was used as a Home Defence night landing ground. Home Defence squadrons had been formed especially to deal with the problems caused by Zeppelin attacks. These squadrons were split into three flights with one, A Flight No 37 (HD), based at Rochford, one at Goldhanger and a third at Stow Maries. 37 Squadron was there to guard the northern part of the Thames Estuary. By the middle of 1916 the coast was better protected as the Army and Navy had improved weaponry with which to defend Southend and the surrounding towns and villages.

Cecil Lewis was a pilot in the Great War and later the author of some fascinating books concerning his time fighting for Great Britain from the skies. He spent a year at Rochford Aerodrome and described it as 'magnificent and almost a mile square.' He joined No 61 Home Defence Squadron, which formed part of the outer defensive ring around London. Pilots were vulnerable in the flimsy flying machines used early in the war and some seemed to have little regard for their own mortality. On one occasion Captain Lewis took a Sopworth Pup on a joy ride to the Isle of White to visit his father. On the way back he became lost in fog with only a compass to find his way back to Rochford. He finally landed in a field but, to his surprise, he was close to Gravesend in Kent rather then being in Essex. Next morning he managed to fly back to Rochford, arriving with almost no petrol left in the tank.

A strange happening was when a Gotha bomber landed at the aerodrome. Apparently the plane had developed engine trouble and, seeing the aerodrome flares, had come in to land, firing a Very Light. Three colours of light were used, red, green and white and the colour was changed each day. The Gotha had somehow fired the right colour, so it was assumed it must be an allied plane. The pilot made an error whilst landing, hit a tree and finally came to rest on the adjacent golf course. The three crew members were taken prisoner, all being unhurt. Officers went out to inspect the wrecked plane and remove the bombs. They also removed the Very Light pistol and cartridges and the Equipment Officer slipped the pistol in his pocket. As he walked away he pulled it out, but the trigger caught in the flap of his pocket and went off. When the plane crashed the fuel tanks had burst and flooded the ground. The magnesium flare from the pistol bounced along the ground towards the plane and within seconds the whole aircraft was engulfed in flames. By morning very little was left of the bomber. If only it had remained intact it would have given invaluable information to investigators, as it was the first of its type to be captured.

As the first half of 1916 drew to a close British Summer Time was introduced. This meant that all clocks were put forward by two hours. It was claimed that hundreds of thousands of tons of coal would be saved by the change. Some farmers objected, but for seaside towns like Southend this must have been a real bonus. The lighter evenings meant that visitors could stay for longer in the town. Clocks would return to normal time in October.

# CHAPTER 5

# No Peace Before Christmas

Almost everyone in England must have known of someone who took part in the carnage of the 1916 Battle of the Somme, and Southend-on-Sea was no exception. Although it was claimed as an Allied victory in the end the cost in human life was colossal. There were almost 60,000 British Expeditionary Force casualties on the first day alone, of whom 20,000 were killed. The battle went on for four and a half

*The British War Medal.* (With thanks to Robert Welham)

months and the final British casualties amounted to some 420,000 men. Yet life at home continued much as it had throughout the war. With no recent aerial attacks on the town there was almost a feeling of complacency. There were the usual worries about the weather and how it would affect the holiday trade; fund raising activities continued and applications were made for deferment from joining the forces for a variety of reasons. The list of those missing in action and those killed grew ever longer in the local newspapers each week.

Conscription had never been popular in the town and, for various reasons, a number of men applied for deferment or exemption. Often employers applied on behalf of employees. Messers White & Co, Builders' Merchants of London Road, Westcliff, made such an application on behalf of a workman named Ives. He was possibly thirty-five and was described as a foreman and telegraph pole maker. Mr White stated that his firm was engaged on army contracts and the tribunal finally agreed to give Ives two months' deferment, presumably while the employer attempted to find a replacement.

Another application for deferment was made by a cattle drover and market porter. His reason for the request was because his father, for whom he worked, was unable to read and write. For this reason he, the son, had to keep the books and was therefore invaluable to his father. After some private deliberation the Tribunal, led by Colonel Newitt, rejected the appeal. Perhaps it was felt that a woman or older man could do this work.

We sometimes forget that Southend was not simply a seaside town. Among other things there were also farms and smallholdings, vital contributors in their own way to the war effort. One was at Eastwood and was owned by Mr Fowler. He applied to the Tribunal to exempt his cowman from service until 1 October. He also requested that a former employee could return to his farm after he had completed his army training. The military representative agreed that this could probably be arranged. He was also told that soldiers would shortly be in the district and if Mr Fowler placed particulars of his needs before the military he might get extra assistance. A ploughman was exempted at the same session. These specialised skills could not be easily replaced, although women were playing an ever more important part in farming, especially following the establishment of the Women's Land Army in 1915.

As more men left for the war it became essential for women to take their places at work. The first female post woman in Southend started her round in April 1916. By early the following year girl messengers were being used by the Southend Post Office to replace boys. Women could also be seen cleaning trains at the town's stations. War was certainly changing the face of the borough in ways that had never been expected.

With imports of food becoming ever more difficult as shipping blockades and submarine attacks continued, prices inevitably rose. In August several thousand trade unionists protested in Hyde Park against the increase in food prices. Yet the people of Southend still gave generously to appeals for both food and money for the military hospitals. A street collection was held in Leigh to raise money for the Victoria Hospital. The previous year the organisers were delighted to collect just over £60. They were worried that donations would be down in 1916 owing to so many claims on the limited resources of their benefactors. However their fears were soon proved to be unfounded as the grand total of over £155 was raised before the end of the day.

There was still thought to be a shortage of land devoted to farming. In November 1916 the government announced that it would take control of any vacant agricultural land to use for the production of food. Even in towns like Southend, small empty plots were converted for the growing of crops. At Southend High School for Boys, situated at Cobweb Corner, land behind it was given over to growing potatoes and peas and also for rearing pigs.

In the autumn of 1916 tanks were first used by the British army, on the Somme. At that time they only had forty-nine of them and some broke down but, when first seen by the enemy, they must have been a terrifying sight.

News of casualties continued to be received at home. One report said that three brothers from West Street, Prittlewell, had been wounded on the same day. They were all riflemen with the Queen's Westminster Rifles. Another local man, Private Arthur G. Ward of the 8th Battalion, Royal Welsh Fusiliers, had been missing since early August and his mother desperately asked if any comrade could supply her with information about his whereabouts. Mrs Carter also requested information about what had happened to her son, Private C. Carter. He had been reported missing some months earlier whilst with the

*An artist's impression of Zeppelin L32.*

Mediterranean Expeditionary Force in Gallipoli. There were many such announcements in the local press, each one bringing a little closer to those at home the true cost of war.

Early in August 1916  it was proudly announced that a Southend man had been awarded the Military Medal. Sergeant F. Spicer of the Essex Regiment, who had served eight months in France, came from Queens Road in the town. He was one of five men from his regiment to receive this award for notable service in the trenches. Before the war he had, for a number of years, been employed by the Midland Railway Company at Southend Station.

The sergeant was not the only man with Southend connexions to be awarded medals for bravery, although only a few can be mentioned in this book. One Southend hero was Corporal Charles Ernest Garforth whose family lived in Tudor Road, Prittlewell. While he was serving with the 15th (The King's) Hussars in the early days of the war his acts of bravery earned him the honour of receiving the Victoria Cross. Under constant fire at Harmingnies the corporal volunteered to cut the wire so that his squadron could escape. A month later, at Dammartin, also in France, he rescued a sergeant who was trapped under his dead horse and the next day he drew off enemy fire for three minutes while another man whose horse had been shot was able to escape. In October he was taken prisoner and remained in captivity or internment until November 1918. He was later promoted to Sergeant. Charles Garforth VC survived the war and eventually died in1973 aged eighty-two.

The pier continued to play an important part in the life of the town.

Although it was used for military activities it was also enjoyed by holiday makers and local residents. There might be a war going on but people still wanted to relax and appreciate the sea air. In the summer of 1916 the Town Clerk reported a complaint from a visitor to the pier regarding the non-working of some automatic machines. The town official sent a letter to the licensee outlining details of the complaint. In his reply the gentleman concerned pointed out that the machines were constantly inspected by his staff and every effort was made to keep them in good working order.

Attention was drawn to another cause for complaint by Councillor Radford. He said that £42 had been spent on supplying water to the pier. This amount was for half a year. The Councillor regarded this as exorbitant and said there must be a great deal of wastage. He suggested that in future only sea water should be used in the lavatories.

Many of the Zeppelins had London as their target, but they would have passed over the Thames Estuary on their way. 1916 saw a number of these attacks. However, defensive measures had greatly improved on the ground and in the air. A large Zeppelin offensive in January 1916 led to lighting restrictions being enforced more vigorously. Although Southend escaped this particular bombardment there were extra warnings about the danger of lights at night, especially near the coast. An early warning system was introduced to herald an impending attack. Air raid warnings became increasingly efficient and there was more co-operation between the use of anti-aircraft guns, searchlights and air defences.

At the end of March 1916 seven Zeppelins attacked London and the south of the country. L13 was hit and damaged early on by anti-aircraft fire. Both L14 and L15 caused damage in Essex, but the latter came under rapid attack from the ground. It was caught in searchlight beams and took a direct hit from one gun, with at least four of its gas cells being damaged. Seventeen aircraft took off to intercept the craft and one, a BE2c, came close. Finally, more than two hours after she had first been hit, the Zeppelin came down in the Thames Estuary. All but one of the crew were rescued and later sent to a Prisoner of War camp. The other man was drowned.

The bad weather that had worried the people of Southend earlier in the year now proved useful. High winds and generally atrocious conditions stopped many of the raids until they recommenced in

September. Then, once again, Zeppelins became more active. Lieutenant William Leefe Robinson, flying a BE2c of 39 Squadron saw the enemy army airship SL11 on its way to central London. A new type of incendiary bullet had been introduced which he used to good effect. The airship caught fire and plunged earthwards. The wrecked remains finally landed in Hertfordshire, much to the delight of the watching onlookers.

At the end of September a new attack on south London by the larger super Zeppelins was planned. L32 was picked out by searchlights and Second Lieutenant Frederick Sowery of 39 Squadron went on the attack. He, too, was flying a BE2c and was using the new incendiary bullets. The airship burst into flames and the wreck landed on a farm in Great Burstead. This was witnessed from as far away as Southend and was well reported in local papers. The entire crew was lost and their remains were buried in the local churchyard. Further raids took place at the beginning of October with more of the great airships being destroyed. Although the Zeppelins continued to be used, most of the attacks in future were by heavy bombers. Many of the attacks on the Zeppelins involved pilots from Rochford Aerodrome, from June 1916 once more in the hands of the Royal Flying Corps. It was used as a Home Defence landing ground and in September as a Flight Station. Home Defence Squadrons were generally used in the fight against Zeppelins.

Numerous ships were sunk during the Great War. One of these was HMS *Zaida,* which went down in the Mediterranean in August 1916. Mr J. Myall, of Hartington Road, Southend had two sons on the ship and believed that both had been lost. However, shortly afterwards he received a letter from his son, Albert, saying that he had been saved and was a prisoner of the Turks. When the ship was hit he had just come off duty and was only wearing his vest. After two and a half hours in the water he was rescued by the enemy. He was in hospital at the time of writing having injured his foot. He added that he had seen nothing of his brother during the action. Later an official notification arrived from the Admiralty, saying that Seaman William Christopher Myall had been lost. He was 24 and an old Brewery Road pupil with a passion for football.

Being an island and not self sufficient in food production and raw materials for industry, Great Britain was very vulnerable to attacks on

*A typical Officers' mess of the Royal Flying Corps.* (By kind permission of Stow Maries Great War Aerodrome)

merchant shipping. As we have seen, where possible every consideration was given to farmers supplying food to the population, with sympathetic consideration being given when local farmers requested deferment for their workers. Many felt that this was as important as serving in the trenches. However the price of many vital commodities continued to rise steadily. In September, 1917 the government suggested, among other considerations, cutting food costs by having one meatless day. How this would have been controlled is hard to imagine. But one price increase that affected everyone was that of bread. Each loaf would, in future, cost ten pence, an exorbitant amount for the poorest families. Bakers claimed that wheat imports had been disrupted by the war and this had led to a rise in the price of flour. Life at home was becoming ever more difficult.

To see why Britain relied so heavily on imported wheat for bread we need to go back to the 1870s and 80s. The weather had been poor for crop growing and, at the same time, cheap wheat from America started flooding the market. Essex was particularly badly hit, with its heavy clay soil which became waterlogged when it rained but baked hard during hot, dry spells. Farmers found it impossible to compete with the low priced imports and much farmland fell into disuse.

Developers moved in. Farms were sold cheaply and some purchased the land and divided it up into small plots. These were advertised in East London with offers to bring prospective purchasers by train to view them. The scheme was a great success and many, for a sum of as little as £10, became land owners for the first time. Former farms that had been sold in this way could not be returned to farming. Although they received no gas, electricity supplies and had no sewage arrangements many of the new owners built bungalows and moved in. The areas developed in this way became known as the Plot Lands. When the war came that land was no longer available for cultivation and, as many merchant ships were sunk, shortages became acute.

Yet even with all these problems the people of Southend still gave keen support to various charity collections, especially those involving help for the wounded in the local hospitals. The Southend and District Automobile Club offered to assist with transport. Colonel and Miss Kember of Runwell Hall invited wounded soldiers and sailors to their home for a third time. Patients went from Queen Mary's Royal Naval Hospital, The Glen, The Overcliff and Victoria Hospitals and also from The Lady Hamilton Convalescent Home. The whole operation was run with military precision. The fleet of cars was due to depart from the various hospitals at 2.15 and 2.30 pm. They arrived at their destination shortly after 3 pm. The men were able to roam around the extensive grounds or play croquet, bowls, clock golf or other outdoor games. After tea they moved inside to be entertained with a concert in the drawing room.

Concerts were very popular at that time and obviously thought suitable for those recovering from war wounds. Another was organized at Stafford Hall in Southchurch Road, when seventy-five soldiers were entertained by the Misses Fergerson and Mr and Mrs Norwell. Afterwards there was a whist drive and, following tea, the visitors joined in with singing and recitations. This gives an interesting glimpse into the type of entertainment that was appreciated at that time.

Although some local people were still able to give generously to charity, others were facing extreme poverty. War was taking its toll on many families, with the main earner no longer at home.

As the year drew towards its close, so did the Battle of the Somme. This was the battle that produced the biggest casualty figures of the war on the Western Front. Amongst the combatants some 1.2 million casualties were suffered, of whom possibly twenty-five per cent were killed, the rest being missing, wounded or prisoners. Such numbers are so huge that they are hard to comprehend. In the light of the losses the government decided that no man under the age of 26 would, in future, be exempted from military service on the grounds of business or employment. The optimism felt at the beginning of the war had vanished.  Neither side had achieved the expected breakthroughs in 1916. In Europe the outlook was grim.

Two songs that were really big hits in 1916 and brought some cheer were 'If you were the only girl in the World' and 'Take me back to dear old Blighty'. These were sung with enthusiasm at the concerts held for wounded soldiers and sailors. However, the third Christmas of the war was described by some sources as 'the bleakest yet.' Would a new year bring more hope? Only time would tell.

# CHAPTER 6

# War at Sea

1917 started badly on a national level. On New Year's Day the Cunard liner *Ivernia* was sunk in the Mediterranean by a German submarine. The reported number feared dead was 153.

Locally, men still appeared before the Tribunals asking for deferment from war service for a variety of reasons. More crops were required to be grown for home consumption, so extra land was needed to be given over to agriculture. The wounded continued to flood into the town's hospitals and various entertainments were organized to keep the men occupied. Irate letters were sent to the local newspapers dealing with various complaints and grievances and the weekly list of those killed or injured fighting abroad continued to grow. Optimism that there would be an early end to the war had all but vanished.

Sometimes official bodies were unable to reach agreement; for example, January saw a disagreement between the military authorities and the Southend Tribunal. This was heard before the War Pensions Committee. The Southend Tribunal had given temporary exemption to twenty-nine year old Mr A.W. Hunt, claiming that it was in the national interest that the employee should remain in his present employment, owing to his indispensability, although what type of work he did was not stated. An appeal was taken to the Central Tribunal which upheld the decision to grant a temporary exemption.

Later in the month another appeal was made concerning a Leigh hairdresser. Apparently that part of the town had been suffering a severe shortage of hairdressers. Mr Banks of Elm Road had appealed for a further deferment extension. After deliberation this was granted until the beginning of May by the Tribunal. Apparently this decision was

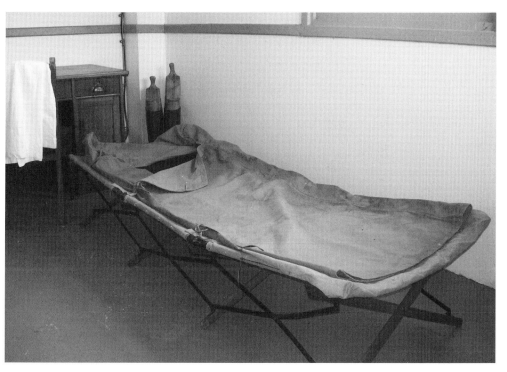

*A Great War camp bed.* (By kind permission of Stow Maries Great War Aerodrome)

greeted with delight by all those from the upper town who had begun to wonder if any skilled hairdresser would be left to deal with their needs. Whether or not this was such a vital occupation that the barber concerned needed deferment is open to debate.

Certainly some work might not at first seem so essential that deferment was necessary. However, Mr Foster of Southchurch Road claimed that a porter in his employment was indispensable to his business. This gentleman had, in fact, been passed as fit for service but Mr Foster claimed that he was now the only man left working in his firm and he was the only one who could cope with much of the work that was too heavy for the female assistants. He was given a two month deferment, as was a tailor aged twenty-four, who had also been passed fit for service abroad.

Southend was not primarily a farming community. Its main harvest, for centuries, had come from the sea. Yet, like other parts of the country, agriculture and increasing yields became ever more important. It has been said, 'An army marches on its stomach'. In some ways this may be true, but those who wait at home also need to be fed. Various directives came from the War Agricultural Committee and sometimes the language was far from clear. A meeting was held early in 1917 to sort out the exact meaning of a statement made by Mr Prothero, President of the Board of Agriculture. This referred to the fixed price of sixty shillings to be paid for wheat by the government. Southend borough farmers were confused. Did the price refer to wheat from 1916 or from 1917? The Chairman assured the meeting that it referred only to 1917 and had nothing to do with that sold in 1916.

The Board of Agriculture was busy at that time. A letter was sent pointing out that the nation expected farmers to grow all the food they possibly could for both human consumption and also for animal stock. Acreage must be increased so that there would be higher yields. Wheat was a necessity and spring wheat should be sown as a priority. Barley was important too and potatoes were absolutely vital. Farmers would be protected by the government against a glut.

To help with waste land cultivation, the Westcliff Society was formed. Southchurch and Leigh already had successful societies organised and the Westcliff group agreed to seek out unused land for this purpose. Often this meant that very small plots were put under cultivation and allotments became popular.

As one way of providing extra food, the medical officer of health suggested that arrangements should be made to grow potatoes in the grounds of the smallpox hospital in Sutton Road. This would help with the supply of food for the patients. The authorities agreed and the land was soon being used to grow crops.

By the beginning of February the Germans stepped up their submarine attacks by declaring an unrestricted campaign. A warning was issued that any ships from neutral countries, trading with the Allies, including the United States, would be torpedoed without warning. This was to have far reaching consequences. When the United States ship *Housatonic* was sunk off Sicily, diplomatic relations with Germany were broken. Later in the month the United States government considered arming their ships against further attacks. At the end of the month the liner *Larconia* was torpedoed. Thirty passengers died, many of them Americans. These attacks on shipping did, however, cause increasing problems in the import of food from abroad. As a result, towns like Southend became ever more dependant on their home grown produce.

*The 1914-1915 Star Medal Presented posthumously to Private C.R. Smith.*
(With thanks to Robert Welham)

Restrictions on street lighting also led to difficulties. A letter to the local paper from a resident complained bitterly about inconsiderate behaviour after dark. He had been walking along Queens Road at night. In attempting to avoid two ladies coming in the opposite direction, he collided with a garden fence that protruded beyond the property boundary and well across the pavement. This resulted in a sprained wrist, a damaged knee, a painful back problem and brief loss of consciousness. The unfortunate gentlemen suggested that kerbs should be whitened, fences controlled and all pedestrians should keep to the right and avoid walking two or three abreast. Whether his recommendations were taken up is not recorded.

Those sent abroad during the war reacted in different ways to their time in foreign lands. The Reverend E. Raymond, curate of St Mary's Prittlewell, wrote home to Canon Dormer to say that he had spent Christmas seventy miles from civilization in the Sinai Desert. He seemed delighted with the situation, pointing out that this was where the caravans of the Patriarchs would have passed, as would the ancient armies of Syria, Assyria, Babylon, Persia, Greece and Rome. Possibly it was also here that the Virgin Mary travelled with Jesus during the flight into Egypt. This experience would obviously be used in the future for a number of sermons!

Food might be scarce but local churches still managed to lay on post Christmas teas and entertainment for the Sunday school children. Gift boxes were also organized for the town's war time hospitals and bandages and other medical needs were collected. Unfortunately not everyone heeded the importance of such collections. Vandals have been around in every age and, sadly, this was true in 1917. The hall of the Shoebury garrison church was broken into on three successive nights and windows were shattered. Finally the thieves managed to get into a room containing parcels ready for dispatch to the Red Cross. Many were opened and those responsible, deciding they were of no monetary value, threw the carefully prepared contents into a ditch, leaving them in a completely useless condition.

In late January news came through of further attacks at sea. An over night destroyer action had taken place off the coast of Holland. Few details were given, but it was stated that British forces met a division of German torpedo boats. One of our destroyers was sunk, but the number of casualties on both sides was not recorded.

There was outrage when it became known that the British hospital ship *Asturias* had been torpedoed by a German submarine. The government described this as 'an unspeakable crime against law and humanity'. The ship had been travelling with its Red Cross signs well illuminated. Thirty-one died and twelve were missing, but there were no wounded on board when the attack happened. The Germans claimed that British hospital ships carried munitions, although this was strongly denied.

Everyone must have known of the high monetary cost of war. There

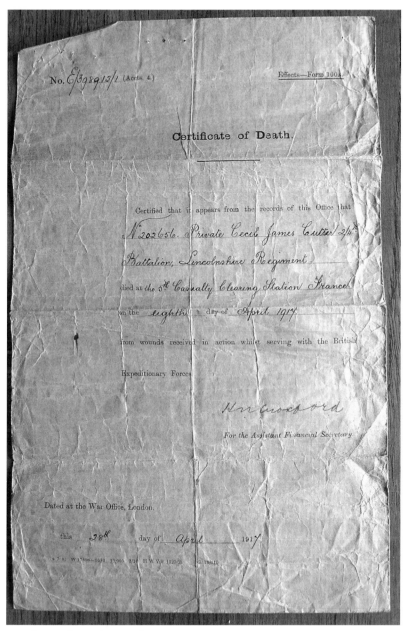

*Death certificate for Cecil James Cutter.*

were frequent appeals for people to purchase War Bonds and letters in the local paper showed how aware some people were that money needed to be saved. One man complained that he had witnessed unnecessary work being done. This involved money being spent that the town could ill afford. He stated that he had seen six men, a horse and van in Eastwood Lane. They were involved in cutting small twigs from young trees. The amount cut was slight and even when the whole lane had been dealt with the cuttings were insufficient to fill the van. He felt sure that another year's growth would have improved the trees for shading purposes. The wages for the men, with the cost of hiring of the horse and van must, he estimated, have amounted to at least £10. He also claimed that, in the same week, he had seen four men with a foreman sweeping up a few leaves. The result of this labour did not fill half a barrow. With the exception of one elderly man, all the workers were apparently able bodied. The Corporation had been forced to write off more than £4,000 in irrecoverable rates and he felt that more economy ought to be practised.

Southenders still vividly recalled the devastating Zeppelin attack on the town in May 1915 when more than one hundred bombs were dropped on the town. It must therefore have been with some delight that they learned of the death of Count Ferdinand von Zeppelin in 1917 at the age of seventy-eight. However, war was changing. Attacks from the air were now mainly by heavy bombers; whilst submarines with their deadly torpedoes, caused death and destruction at sea. As more ships were sunk, many of them belonging to the United States, America made preparations for serious retaliation. In April 1917 President Woodrow Wilson signed a declaration of war against Germany. This was to have a major impact on the future conduct of the conflict.

Newspapers were full of accounts of the battles in Europe and beyond. Those fighting were described as heroes and young boys often played with mock swords and guns. This led to a very sad case in the town. Forty year old Miss Louisa Burrow Walker lived in Eastwood Road, near the borough boundary. She had been shopping in Leigh and on her return home was approached from behind and shot with a revolver. She died shortly afterwards.

Although there were no witnesses to the murder a youth from Hadleigh was soon arrested and put on trial, found guilty and sentenced to death. His actual age was not given. However, the judge supported a plea for leniency in view of the young age of the murderer, but a long prison sentence was inevitable. How the boy acquired the gun is unknown.

On a lighter note a Red Cross working party, set up at the beginning of the war, met every Thursday in Leigh. These ladies obviously worked with great enthusiasm. In the previous year they had made sixty pairs of pyjamas, sixty-nine shirts, ninety-three pillow cases, one pair of bed stockings, three pairs of cuffs, one pair of pants, a scarf, twenty-three bandages, four dusters and one single sheet! Many of these items were sent to the hospitals although one bundle of new garments was sent to a school to be given to poor children and a parcel was also sent to a soldier's widow. Poverty was a very real problem in some parts of the town. The group made a plea for donations towards their funds and materials that could be used for their future work.

*Charles Marriot in Merchant Seaman's uniform.* (With thanks to Susan Marriott Yarwood)

Letters sent home still flowed in from those serving in France and further afield. Parents expressed concern about sons reported as missing and asked for anyone with information to get in touch. The 4th Battalion of the Essex Volunteer Regiment appealed for 1,000 men to join the Southend Battalion for the duration of the war. Uniform and equipment would be supplied free to all applicants. Meanwhile there was still an ever growing list of local casualties from the war zones.

As the submarine attacks grew in intensity the shortage of food became ever more apparent. There was an acute shortage of flour and in May a royal proclamation was issued in which the King called for a national effort to reduce the consumption of bread. The royal household had been on strict rations since February in their own effort to cut back. People were asked to avoid using flour in pastry, although what was to be used instead was not reported. The shortage of potatoes was also growing ever more serious and every available spare plot was being brought into use for growing vegetables.

The armed services were sometimes forced to get involved in non military activities. On Whit Sunday 1917, visitors to Thorpe Bay were confronted with the sight of the carcass of a horse being brought in by the tide. Two months previously a Foulness farmer and his horse had disappeared and now the mystery was solved. They had drowned at sea. The weather was fine and the carcass remained close to the promenade throughout the day. Then, as the evening tide came in, a Naval launch appeared to tow it out to sea, where presumably it was weighted down to prevent the same problem occurring again.

It has been mentioned previously that a list was being drawn up of all local men serving with the colours. By May 1917 this had reached more than 12,000 names. A request was made for yet more information to be given and a decision that any changes in rank should be recorded along with any new honours received. As many more men had signed on since the Derby Scheme and the Military Service Act were introduced, it was felt it was likely that a number of names had been omitted.

On 14 June the first raids by German heavy bombers were made on London's East End. With approximately fifteen aircraft involved, the raid lasted for just fifteen minutes, but in that time more than one hundred were killed and another four hundred injured. Ten children were killed when one bomb landed on a school. The war had entered yet another new phase. Previous attacks had been made by Zeppelins, which were fairly easy targets, but the bombers were far more difficult to attack. All too soon Southend was to know the horror that the heavy bombers could unleash.

As the first half of 1917 drew to a close the situation in Europe was changing. The first American troop ships arrived off the French coast in late June. In the United States great numbers rushed to join the colours, But it would take about a year for them to be trained and to arrive on the Western Front in any significant numbers, but eventually they were bound to have an enormous impact. News from the front was depressing, but some new optimism must have been felt at the news of this great boost to the numbers of those involved in the war.

# CHAPTER 7

# Death from the Skies

By mid 1917 Southend residents were really feeling the effects of wartime restrictions. Many committees continued to meet, covering all aspects of everyday life. Collections were made of both goods and money to help the local military hospitals and also for the troops serving overseas. Prestigious visitors came, including HRH Princess Mary. She went to Queen Mary's Royal Naval Hospital in June to be present and receive donations at a mid-week Gift Day. Among the articles donated were thirty-three large towels made by members of the Shoeburyness Working Party. These ladies had been very busy also

*Memorial to Lieutenant Oswald Griffith RFA to be found at Westborough School.* (With thanks to Heather Feather)

making pyjamas, bed jackets, handkerchiefs and operation stockings. Even in summer bed jackets were necessary in large wards where there was little or no auxiliary heating.

In the Great War the slaughter at the front reached proportions never before experienced or ever imagined possible. Yet for each man lost there was a wife, mother or family members who also suffered. There was a local War Pensions Committee which hoped 'to enlist the sympathy and assistance of ladies with time at their disposal'. It was envisaged that these women would visit the wives and dependants of those in the town serving with the forces. There was also an appeal for co-operation from employers to help men to find work once they were discharged from the forces.

The War Pensions Committee came into existence in the previous July at the behest of the Naval and Military War Pensions Act of 1915. Its purpose was to continue the work of the National Relief Fund. It was expected to distribute supplementary allowances and grants to the wives and dependants of soldiers and sailors serving in the war and to the widows and dependants of those who had lost their lives, or those who were medically unfit to continue serving. The support was largely of a temporary nature and would continue only for the duration of the war or until demobilization.

Although air raids continued on London and the war persisted overseas the people of Shoebury were once again thinking about a war memorial to honour those who had died. Temporary memorials were erected, to be replaced after the war by permanent structures. It was suggested that a small committee should be formed with a treasurer to start collecting subscriptions. The chairman felt sure that money would come in, although he complained about the poor attendance at the meeting. Sadly the weekly list of those killed in action continued to be sizeable. One of those included was Second Lieutenant H.A. Hope of Manor Road, Westcliff. He had been on patrol in France and met with an accident to his aircraft when landing at the end of his mission. He was killed on 28 July 1917.

August was the time for special treats for the children. There were Sunday School outings and special events for the boy scouts. The Empire Theatre had faced many previous problems but it had been re-decorated, re-seated and renovated. It was also described as having adequate ventilation and general comfort. At that time there was

*Alfred and Agnes Carter (née Brewer) on their wedding day, 25 December,
1920. They witnessed the devastation caused by the 12 August 1917 bombing.*
(With thanks to Sylvia Harrington)

obviously no fear of possible war damage in the minds of those involved, but on 12 August 1917 everything changed.

The weather was cloudy but fine. Being a Sunday it was a good day for holiday makers to make a day trip to the town. Trains were running and it was an easy journey from east London to the beaches of Southend. Traders were set to have a profitable day. By late afternoon, tired but happy visitors began to wend their way along the High Street towards the town's two railway stations.

At around 5 pm a flight of nine Gotha aeroplanes was seen approaching Felixstowe. They belonged to the 3rd Battle Squadron and were commanded by Oberleutnant Walther. No 61 Squadron was on alert, but ordered to stay on the ground as it was believed that the intended target was London. There were already other allied planes in the air and this may have caused the German plans to be revised. The Battle Squadron changed course, heading for Rochford and ultimately Southend. The station commander at Rochford Aerodrome, ignoring orders, immediately had his squadron airborne. Two 50 kilogramme bombs were dropped on the aerodrome and two men of the Royal Flying Corps were injured.

As No 61 Squadron tried to force the enemy planes to fly higher, the Germans broke formation and flew towards Canvey Island, Leigh, Westcliff and Southend, dropping bombs as they went. In the town the pavements were crowded with those making their way to the station. Many were holiday makers returning home and others were church goers. Most people seemed unworried by the planes as they approached. They were flying low so they believed them to be British. Then the bombs started falling. One fell close to the Central Station. A woman was injured and a number of shop windows shattered. The force of the blast blew two people through an empty shop doorway and a boy was killed, with others being injured. Another 50 kilogram bomb fell close to the Technical School at Cobweb Corner. Although windows in the building were shattered, there were no casualties.

When another 50 kilogram bomb fell in Victoria Avenue, close to the Great Eastern Railway Station, later known as Southend Victoria, the result was very different. Fifteen people were killed and others maimed in the explosion. Some believed the target to be the station itself, but this survived. The raid lasted for just fifteen minutes, but the result was devastating. Thirty-two people were killed that day, ten men,

*Florence Emma Gowers, 1904-2001, who witnessed the aftermath of the 12 August 1917 air raid.* (With thanks to Vic Knight)

thirteen women and nine children. Forty-three were injured, thirteen of them men, eighteen women and twelve children. Of the dead, fifteen were residents and seventeen visitors. The majority of these were close to the station, although nine died in the Milton Street area, six in Guildford Road and two in Lovelace Gardens.

Sylvia Harrington vividly remembers the stories her grandmother, Agnes Carter, née Brewer, told. Agnes was just 19 at the time and she often talked of that terrible day in the years to follow. She was with Alfred, her future husband. They were returning from the seafront to the station in Victoria Avenue, ready to catch a train to Wickford. Before they reached their destination the bomb had dropped and she recalled Alfred gallantly putting his hands over her eyes to cut out the sight of the blood and mutilated bodies lying on the ground.

Florence Emma Gowers, later Knight, also witnessed the carnage. Her son, Vic Knight, recalls her memories of that time. She possibly arrived on the scene a little later than Sylvia's grandmother, because she remembered bread baskets being brought out from Garons' bakery for the collection of body parts. She was 13 at the time but the memory of that awful day remained with her until she died in 2001.

Although many of the visitors were on their way home there were also local church goers in the area. One little girl was on her way to a Salvation Army meeting. A mother lost her life, although her two children, who were with her at the time, survived. An aerial torpedo destroyed a house in Guildford Road and two occupants were killed, although three others were later rescued from a cupboard beneath the staircase of the house. Such cupboards were often used for safety in the days before purpose built shelters were available. Part of the torpedo was found lodged between the chimneys of a house opposite. Several bombs fell on allotments. Later it was discovered that some of the vegetables, including potatoes, had been blown by the force of the impact out of the ground and through the broken windows of nearby houses. The request to use all available land for cultivation had obviously been heeded.

The raiders quickly gained height and escaped towards the sea where they dropped their remaining bombs. Anti-aircraft guns were fired and British planes gave chase. It was reported that two German planes were destroyed, a seaplane and a Gotha bomber. Later it was learned that a dog and a horse were both killed, the latter belonging to a greengrocer in Leigh Road. It was hit by fragments flying from a bomb that had fallen in Grasmere Road. Fortunately, although some property was damaged, there were no human deaths in Leigh, although seven cows grazing in a field near London Road, Leigh, met a similar fate to the dog and horse. The ages of those killed that day ranged from 6 to 74.

Bodies were quickly removed and shops with shattered windows were boarded up. Yet on that August evening sightseers and relic hunters soon gathered. In fact there were so many that the police and special constables had difficulty keeping the traffic moving. Fairly quickly life in the town returned to normal, but for many friends,

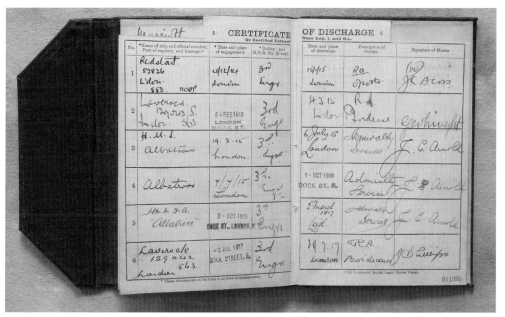

*Certificate of Discharge for Charles Marriott.* (With thanks to Susan Marriott Yarwood)

families, children and those who had seen the results, that brief time of bombing changed their lives for ever.

The late Arthur Hance, when talking to his granddaughter Karen Boyd, née Hance, recalled seeing strange lights in the sky during the war, although the exact date is uncertain. There were a number of reports of unusual lights being seen during the war. He said, 'One night during or just after an air raid the whole northern sky glowed and my parents thought that German bombers had succeeded in setting the whole town of Chelmsford on fire but, in the morning, the papers reported that there had been a display of the "Northern Lights" or, to give it its scientific name, Aurora Borealis. That is the only time I have seen it.'

At the front, by the end of August, the Third Battle of Ypres had gone on for some four weeks. The weather was horrendous, with endless rain turning the already muddy fields into even more of a quagmire. Some were unsure whether they were more afraid of the German bombardment or of the mud. If a man slipped from the duckboards placed across the ground there was a good chance of being lost in the hopelessly boggy terrain.

Food shortages continued and imported sugar became very scarce. By order of the food controller, shop keepers asked their customers to fill in a form, which included their name, address and number in the family. This was to be returned to the retailer so that the sugar ration could be distributed fairly.

As the town recovered from the shock of the devastating bomb attack of 12 August, local charity workers did their best to maintain an air of normality. Mr Maitland Keddie arranged for the wounded to be collected from the Queen Mary Royal Naval Hospital with others from the Glen Hospital. They were to be taken for an outing to Thundersley Rectory. Arrangements were made with military precision and there were the usual entertainments laid on for the visitors. Another group was welcomed by Colonel and Miss Kemble at Runwell Hall and, later in the year, Mr and Mrs Cecil of Rayleigh Lodge entertained wounded sailors in their home. Once again Mr Maitland Keddie was responsible for the arrangements.

Many women were left in straitened circumstances without the main breadwinner when the men in the family went to war. The weekly lists of those killed or seriously wounded grew and making ends meet must have been an ever increasing problem for a growing number of those at home. Without the National Health Service we now enjoy, even slight illnesses could quickly escalate into major problems. It is easy to forget that the Poor Law was still in existence during the war, although its use had declined during the early years of the twentieth century. It had functioned from late–medieval and Tudor times but was not finally abolished until 1948, with the passing of the National Assistance Act. Even then, some parts remained until 1967. In Southend a doctor was still appointed under the Poor Law to deal with patients who were unable to pay for medical help. A series of letters appeared in the local paper, some berating local doctors for being unwilling to deal with  these people but others pointing out that many medical men gave their time and skills willingly to help those less fortunate than themselves. One writer sternly objected to those who criticized all doctors without first checking the facts.

Conscription continued and some Southend men or their employers continued to apply for deferment. In September, Mr Osborne, a coal merchant, appealed on behalf of his coal loader who worked in Leigh, claiming that he was in an essential occupation. The tribunal suggested that Mr Osborne could himself do the loading, but the employer argued that he was unfit to do such work and if his loader did not get exemption then many people would go without coal. In the end the man was simply granted two months' temporary exemption.

Early in September there was an attack just across the Thames from Southend, with horrendous results. One hundred and eight people were killed in an air raid on the Isles of Sheppey and Thanet. From the Western Front news came of a German attack on Allied hospitals, resulting in the killing of a number of Americans.

Private James Warr of the Essex Regiment, who lived in Ruskin Avenue, Southend, had been wounded but returned once more to the front line. There he received appalling injuries, resulting in the loss of both legs. In spite of this disaster his letters home remained surprisingly cheerful and he looked forward to returning to the town once more. Another local man who had a shrapnel wound to his left wrist made the very British comment that the weather was probably the main factor in prolonging the war. He felt that this had contributed to the fact that the allies were not yet enjoying complete success.

Southend had its own Food Control Committee. It advertised for the services of a competent man with a good knowledge of accounts, book keeping and food. Presumably this would either be an older man or one wounded and discharged from war service. He was to work under the direction of the executive officer. His appointment was to last for the duration of the war and for some time afterwards. Notice of one month on either side would be necessary. The successful applicant would be paid £3 per week and he needed to state his qualifications and supply three testimonials. One must wonder how many people actually applied. Apparently women were not to be considered.

Entertainment was always important, even close to the front. One officer was reported as saying, "It takes a great deal of effort, but we might have lost the war if it had not been for the laughter." At home too there was a great attempt to keep the wounded from the hospitals in good spirits. There was a Charity Entertainments Committee, with Mr Fred Donnithorne as the secretary. He had been under pressure to organize matinees and, although his work made this difficult, he decided to take over the Hippodrome on 5 December 1917 for this purpose. Profits from the previous year had gone to the Queen Mary Royal Naval Hospital, so the new profits would go to the Glen, followed by the Overcliff. Mr Donnithorne had already been busy making arrangements and proudly announced that the renowned singer, Miss Clara Tubb, had agreed to visit the town to perform on that occasion.

As the war in Europe continued so did aerial attacks on England. Some Zeppelins were still involved and eight attacked London in October, killing twenty-seven. However, these craft were now more vulnerable than they were earlier in the war, as defensive weapons had improved greatly. Four of the craft were destroyed over France as they made their way home to Germany.

Although there had been no further disastrous attacks on Southend since the August air raid, there was a fear that there might be further troubles in the coming year. It was suggested that the construction of adequate shelters should be a priority. Some private businesses had already been offering shelter on their premises during air raids to those in need. Mr Geoffrey Phillips, of Satanita Road, Westcliff suggested that soldiers in the area might be used to dig dugouts for use as shelters. This could be used as part of their training and civilians could be used to help too. Girls could make sand bags whilst the men would do the more strenuous work. As the year drew to an end little more was heard of this suggestion.

1917 had certainly been a memorable one for the town. On one level life continued much as it had before. Yet the events of 12 August must have had a great impact on everyone living in Southend at that time. Before that day there may have been a feeling of complacency. Time had passed since the last two attacks by Zeppelins. Now they knew that the danger was ever present and it must have been a most uncomfortable feeling.

# CHAPTER 8

# Shortages and Inflation

By the early months of 1918 shortages were causing real problems. With the many torpedo attacks on allied shipping, goods from abroad had become increasingly difficult to obtain. The supply of food was a real problem. In January, London restaurants and eating houses were ordered by the government to refrain from serving meat on two days each week and in Southend the local Food Control Committee agreed to set up a central kitchen to supply cooked meals.

The idea of the kitchen was that anyone, of whatever social status, would be able to buy meals during the time of acute food shortages. These were not replacements for the earlier charity run soup kitchens. They were co-operatives set up to supply food to both rich and poor at their own expense. There was obviously some concern that potential customers would feel demeaned if they attended the kitchen, but it was pointed out that there would be no loss of self-respect for anyone who decided to eat there. Profit making would not be a consideration. In fact the institutions were to be completely self-sufficient. The Southend Municipal Kitchen opened in Queens Road and was so successful that the people of Leigh soon decided that they would like something similar.

There was still a big problem with meat shortages. On one Saturday, when over one thousand portions were served in the Southend kitchen, the main savoury dish was mock goose. This consisted of potato, onions and various other non-meat ingredients and it was described as 'delicious'. The dessert dish was rice pudding, but one woman insisted on having her rice put directly on top of the mock goose. The local

*Westborough School, opened 1912.*

paper said, 'It is pleasing to note that all classes were represented among the clients.' Vegetable sausages became popular at this time.

Meat shortages continued. News spread quickly and queues formed as soon as a butcher's shop had even a small supply. Most of the proprietors tried to keep the majority of their limited supply for regular customers. This happened in Leigh on the Broadway, but shops that were without meat pulled down their blinds and locked the doors. For many the traditional joint was missing from the table on a Sunday.

Dissatisfaction grew and it was felt that the local Food Committee did not represent all classes of society. Women were liable to stand for hours in queues to obtain even a small supply of necessary items such as meat and edible fats and it was not unusual for stocks to be exhausted before everyone could be served. Some disgruntled rail men threatened to take the place of women in the queues and this would cause considerable disruption to traffic. The Food Committee met but, according to a newspaper reporter, they talked and talked for two hours yet made little progress!

Some shop proprietors took matters into their own hands by

producing their own rationing system in anticipation of a government scheme to follow. Those who wished to do so could list their names for tea, butter and margarine and if any was available they would get preference. The distribution was only done very roughly and each registered family, regardless of size, received the same amount. Even so, most people felt relieved that some effort was being made to help the situation.

Another problem in 1918 was the colossal cost of the war. Everyone was encouraged to buy War Bonds; the highest numbers sold in the town were to Southend High School for Boys, St Saviour's Church and Westborough School. As we have seen, Southend, throughout the war, responded well to calls for financial support. One advertisement for the International Stores suggested two ways to help the war effort: first, buy more National War Bonds, which could be obtained from post offices for £5 upwards; the second solution was to change breakfast habits by drinking coffee instead of tea. Both tea and coffee were imported, but there seems to have been a much greater demand for the former, so stocks ran low. Whether or not this suggestion was successful seems doubtful.

In times when most properties have central heating it is easy to

*Priory Park gates.*

forget the problems that could be caused by frozen pipes. In January a very sharp frost was followed by a rapid thaw. Many houses faced the worry of burst pipes, causing considerable damage to furniture and walls. This caused great concern in Leigh. Most plumbers had long since been called up for war service. Only one or two skilled men remained and they were incapable of dealing with the sudden increase in demand for their services. Some leaks remained unstopped for a considerable time and a number of houses had the water supply cut off. The only solution was to find more fortunate neighbours willing to allow others to collect water from their taps. No one seemed to foresee the problems that might be caused by allowing skilled young plumbers to be enlisted, but this was a concern that must have been experienced throughout the country.

On a more cheerful note the special matinees arranged in aid of the military hospitals continued. These were held at the Hippodrome and appear to have been highly successful. The Mayor, Alderman Joseph Francis, attended one in late January, accompanied by his wife. Other local dignitaries were also present, giving the event an added feeling of importance. Money was raised on that occasion for the Overcliff Hospital. The children of a local Baptist Church, instead of having their usual post Christmas party and tea, gave a concert on behalf of the Red Cross Society. Both the children and the audience thoroughly enjoyed the experience.

A number of Southend men belonged to the Volunteer Training Corps, which acted as a type of home guard. Members were mainly those over military age or in occupations that gave them exemption from normal war service. They did not have weapons at first, although they used dummy weapons for drill purposes. Although in its earliest days the Corps was not officially recognised, by November 1914 it was taken under the wing of the War Office. The units had to be self supporting and provide their own uniforms, although these could not be khaki. Lovat green was the preferred colour. Under the Volunteer Act of 1863 the men could give fourteen days notice of their intention to resign, but it was soon realised that this option was a weakness in time of war.

With the introduction of conscription in 1916, the Military Service Tribunals were able to order men to join the Voluntary Training Corps, but the fourteen day resignation clause was quickly altered by the passing of the Volunteer Act and members were then expected to belong until the end of the war. From 1917 they could carry weapons and were expected to take part in a certain number of drills. They wore red arm bands bearing the letters GR, standing for Georgius Rex. However, various wits decided that the initials stood for George's Wrecks, Grandpa's Regiment, Genuine Relics or Government Rejects! They were able to tackle a number of tasks, including the guarding of vulnerable places, fire fighting, digging anti-invasion defence lines and transporting wounded soldiers. In 1918 they took on a three month coastal defence duty in East Anglia, a vital role when so many men were fighting overseas. The Corps was finally suspended in December, 1918 and officially disbanded in January 1920.

There was still a long list of men who applied for deferment from serving in the forces for a variety of reasons. Some were successful, but with ever greater need for soldiers to fight at the front, many were not.

With increasing shortages prices rose. The *Southend Standard* announced in February that it was reluctantly being forced to raise its

*Plaque beside Priory Park gates.*

price from a penny to one and a half pence. The proprietor pointed out that nearly one thousand daily and weekly newspapers had already increased their prices. This was owing to increased restrictions and the rising cost of paper. The only alternative was to reduce the size of the paper, something they were very reluctant to do.

Admission prices for the pier were also rising. The toll had been one penny, but this was to go up to two. The fee for admission to the pier extension was to increase and on Bank Holidays, Sundays and those mornings when the band was playing the price at the pier head would also rise. Whether this affected the number of those using this facility is not recorded, but we do know that when public tram fares were also increased the number using them dropped steeply and little extra money was raised from the change in price.

Returning to the subject of food, efforts to use even small plots of land for growing vegetables were proving to be very successful. By March the Leigh Land Cultivation Society reported that they were delighted with the results from their propaganda. There had been an increase in membership and more plots were being used, but they were still not satisfied. The committee decided to arrange house to house visits to make sure that everyone capable of digging and planting was already cultivating a plot. If not, then the callers were to endeavour to persuade them to start doing so at once. There was certainly no lack of enthusiasm among the committee members.

After the gloomy news of shortages in January, by March some shops were beginning to advertise supplies of butter, margarine and other edible fats. In fact meat, butter and margarine rationing had started in late February. Although the displays might look inviting, only registered customers were able to purchase the goods on display.

In April a new Military Service Bill received the Royal Assent. This was the fifth version of the Act, the first being in January 1916. The most notable provision of the recent amendment was that men aged 17 to 51 could be called up. This caused much dissatisfaction in Southend. Previously the cut off age had been 41. It was reported that some members of the tribunal dealing with the new conscription rules resigned, being unwilling to send men of their own age or older into the army. Most people had firmly believed that 41 would remain the top age limit, but the situation on the Western Front, meant that ever more men were needed.

Local farmers and market gardeners were also worried by the new Act, wondering how they would be affected by the withdrawal of exemption. An advertisement suggested that immediate application should be made to the County Agricultural Executive Committee, asking for a certificate for any men who were highly skilled and employed full time and were essential to the running of the farm or smallholding. If a certificate was granted, then the Appeal Tribunal would consider the case and possibly grant exemption. On no account should anyone delay in making the initial application.

There continued to be many reports of men from the town killed or wounded. Also the names of those who received military awards were recorded. Mr and Mrs Carey had lost three sons in the conflict, first Private Stanley Carey of the Essex Regiment and later two more of the brothers, Albert and Sydney, both riflemen. Previously, Sydney had been wounded twice. It is hard to imagine the impact of such news on the parents of the three men. There was a more encouraging report

*Jones Memorial Ground gate and dedication.*

saying that Lieutenant (Acting Captain) J. Cagin of the London Regiment and formerly of Warrior Square, Southend, had been awarded the Military Cross for conspicuous gallantry and devotion to duty. When in command of three companies he went forward under heavy fire to reinforce the left battalion. This was in a critical situation at that time. He made suitable dispositions and established a strong line of defence.

At the beginning of April the Royal Flying Corps and the Royal Naval Air Service were merged into the new Royal Air Force. Throughout the war airman did sterling work to protect the country from enemy attack. All too often this resulted in loss of life. Rochford Aerodrome continued to play a vital part in the war effort.

The ladies of Southend and district continued to give what support they could to those fighting at the front and the wounded who arrived at the local hospitals. The local Needlework Guild proudly reported that they had passed on seventy-two shirts, twenty pairs of socks, four mufflers and four cardigans. Some of these items were sent to Lieutenant P.W. Wilde of the Tank Corps for distribution amongst his men. It mentioned that some items collected were disinfected, presumably because they were second hand and had possibly been repaired by the Guild before distribution.

The Mayor of Southend proposed that there should be a united memorial service for all the local men who had fallen. He felt that any such service must be of a united character as the men and their families had very different backgrounds and beliefs. He thought that such a service would be appreciated by relatives and also by the men who were still serving. As so many were still dying the list of the fallen was kept open until well after the war ended.

Long before Southend existed as a town there was a village to the north known as Prittlewell. It was here, in the twelfth century, that Cluniac monks from the Priory of St Pancras at Lewes in Sussex, founded their own priory. It continued until the dissolution of the monasteries under Henry VIII, when it passed into private hands. In 1536 much of the building was destroyed and the rest was greatly altered. Finally, in 1917 it was bought by a local jeweller, Mr R.A. Jones.

Robert Arthur Jones was born in Liverpool in 1849. After working as a clock and watch maker he moved to Southend and, in 1890 opened a jewellery business in the High Street. This was highly successful and he became a major benefactor to the town. It is easy to forget that shops, other than those selling food, continued to operate during the Great War.

In 1913 Robert Jones presented the Jones Memorial Ground to the town in memory of his wife. This was for the use of the school children of the town. Later he purchased Prittlewell Priory complete with twenty-two acres of land. He also bought another six acres to add to the site. The Priory and the surrounding land was then presented to the town to be used as a park. The old Priory building was to become a museum. He once said, "I think it is a sin for any man to die rich. It is a great privilege for me to do this, for I strongly believe in facilities for recreation." This park remains one of the most beautiful in the town and is a reminder that, even in the middle of the most terrible war in the history of mankind to that date, there is still a need for a place of peace and tranquillity, and this can certainly be found in Priory Park.

R.A. Jones died in 1925 and his son, Edward Cecil Jones, took over the High Street store and continued his father's good works. He had been a hero of the Great War and was awarded the Military Cross. On two occasions he was sent home after being wounded, but returned to the front as soon as possible after a period of convalescence. He once described the winter of 1916-17 as the worst one could possibly imagine and conditions on the Somme as being awful beyond description. The town owes a great debt of gratitude to both R.A. Jones and his son. The name of the latter is still remembered in the title of the Cecil Jones School.

# CHAPTER 9

# End Game

In 1918 a crippling world wide influenza pandemic known as Spanish flu resulted in so many deaths across Europe and the rest of the world that the total was greater than those who were lost in the war. Wartime censors, worried about the effect on morale if the full extent of the crisis became known, minimized the seriousness of the problem in early reports, as did those in Germany, France and the United States. Spain remained neutral during the war and so uncensored reporting was allowed. Because of this it appeared that Spain was especially badly hit by the flu and so it became known as Spanish flu. It was said to have caused a month long lull in fighting on the Western Front, though this is somewhat fanciful, as the German Spring offensive had run out of steam. Fierce fighting resumed in July and some reports concluded that the tide was turning in favour of the Allies. As an increasing number of Americans arrived, there was real hope.

At home life went on much as before. The government had introduced fixed price controls on a number of items, including footwear. Jennings, one of the leading shoe shops with stores in various parts of the town, advertised that they had in stock children's boots and shoes. These were described as being made from H form lasts, had good uppers and soles and were sold at fixed, government controlled prices. However, another trader ignored the price controls and was summoned under the Defence of the Realm Act, Confectionary Order 6. His crime had been to sell Rock at a price exceeding 2d per ounce. This was always a popular confectionary in the town, especially enjoyed by children, and the vendor was obviously exploiting the market.

*Pilots' Ready Room, where they waited to be scrambled for flight.* (By kind permission of Stow Maries Great War Aerodrome)

Another case where restrictions were ignored concerned a naturalized German. He was charged at Southend Police Court with unlawfully acquiring food in excess of the amount required for ordinary consumption. For this offence he was held on remand.

Some of the shortages felt earlier in the year had eased, but restrictions were still rigorously upheld. The need for home grown food remained and the local allotment societies continued to work with enthusiasm. There was some concern about potato disease and the producer of a product known as Bergercide advertised that the yield of each plant could be increased by two and a half per cent if it was mixed with water and sprayed.

Reports still appeared regularly telling of the bravery of local men. Lieutenant E. Cryd, formerly of Westcliff, was mentioned in dispatches by General Plumer. This was for distinguished and gallant service and devotion to duty in Italy. Lieutenant D.H. Roberton of the RAF took

*The late Bernard Riley, who remembered the German Officers' Prisoner of War Detention centre in Victoria Avenue.*

part in what was described as 'an exciting raid' on a town behind the German lines. He had unloaded his bombs when he was attacked by ten aircraft. At the time he was on his return journey and was taking photographs. In spite of bullet wounds in his arm and thigh and shrapnel in his back he succeeded in shooting down two of the enemy planes, although his own aeroplane was badly damaged. Somehow he still managed to return home to safety. At the time of the report he was recovering locally.

To receive notification that a loved one was missing was obviously devastating. Mrs Tune, of Princes Street, Southend, received such a message in March 1918. Her son was F. Tune, a signaller of the Essex Regiment. Then a card and letter arrived from her son in July to say that he was in fact a prisoner of war in Germany. Another mother receiving a similar message was Mrs Wenden, of St Anne's Road, Southend. Private S. Wenden of the Royal Fusiliers had also been missing since March but, like Private Tune, was a prisoner of war in Germany and was apparently quite well.

In the spring of 1918 five officers' prisoner of war camps were opened, one of which was in Southend. These were close to sensitive installations in areas that were vulnerable to air attacks. Some believed that this action was taken because the Germans had moved allied prisoners into dangerous areas close to the battle lines. The late Bernard Riley had an early memory of a prison camp in Victoria Avenue, not far from the railway station. This was an obvious potential target. He was travelling along the road on the top deck of a tram. At that time there were some large houses lining the street, most with substantial gardens. He looked down on one that was surrounded by a high wall. From his elevated position he was able to see prisoners walking around, guarded by sentries; these were German officer prisoners of war. The house was called Bellfields and was later used as a school for pupils of Westcliff High Schools, both for boys and girls. The Civic Centre now stands on the site.

Most of those serving in the war wore their uniforms with pride. Unfortunately, there will always be some who use uniform as a disguise to hide criminal activities. Such a man was John Raynor, a twenty-two year old who dressed himself in the uniform of a naval officer. He managed to steal a number of articles from the home of Mrs Smith of Southend. He was arrested on Whit Sunday, still in Southend, and was

*Memorial to two former pupils of Westborough School.* (With thanks to Heather Feather)

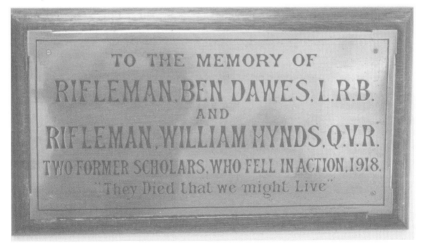

found to have a revolver in his possession. At his subsequent trial he was found guilty and sentenced to eighteen months hard labour. At the end of the day he was sent, with other prisoners, to London's Liverpool Street Station. At that point three of the prisoners were removed, ready to be taken to Pentonville. Raynor was to go to Brixton, where he was to appear before the Middlesex Quarter Sessions on further charges. He was handcuffed but, as the other prisoners were being removed, he saw his chance and escaped into a dense crowd. At the time of the report he was still at large.

The Corri family lived in Seaforth Road, Westcliff. The father, Mr Eugene Corri, was a well known and much respected boxing referee. His eldest son, Midshipman Eugene Corri, was educated at Lindisfarne College and joined the Cunard Steamship Company at the age of 14. By that time he had already travelled widely when his father went to boxing tournaments. In 1918 he was serving aboard HMHS *Llandovery Castle* of the Union-Castle Line. This was a Canadian hospital ship on a voyage from Halifax, Nova Scotia to Liverpool. On 27 June it was close to southern Ireland when it was torpedoed by SM U-86. In all 234 lives were lost and there were only twenty-four survivors. Firing at a hospital ship broke international law and the standing orders of the German Navy.

Some details of the death of the teenager later appeared in the *Liverpool Post*. Charles Gregory was a survivor from the ship. He described how some of the men were in an open boat riding on swelling seas in a storm. Suddenly a wave broke over them and carried away the youngest member of the crew. They could hear him calling and just once they saw his face before a huge wave broke over him. Rescue was impossible. One report said he was 16 and a half, but another claimed he was 17. Either way he was a very young victim of the cruelty of war.

The town still welcomed important visitors intent on raising money and gifts for the military hospitals. An early announcement said that the Duchess of Portland would be visiting the Queen Mary Royal Naval Hospital in July. Early booking to attend was essential as there were also to be water sports and various other activities. It was later reported that the day had been extremely successful, although the weather had not been kind. The money raised was to buy extra comforts for the hospital patients.

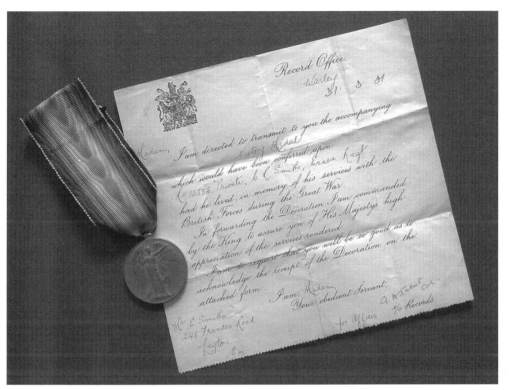

*The Victory Medal.* (With thanks to Robert Welham)

In May the government abolished compulsory meatless days and in June there was the introduction of General Rationing. All ration books for which application had been made at the correct time were to be in the hands of householders by 12 July 1918. Late applications would be dealt with speedily. There was a problem, however, because although the books had been prepared a week earlier the special instruction leaflet that should have been included was delivered late. Another problem was caused by the fact that 3,000 householders had failed to insert their addresses when filling in the application form and 5,000 had failed to make any application at all. According to the local newspaper report, this had caused congestion in the office and overtaxed the energies of the staff who were attempting to deal with the situation.

The Southend Food Control Committee was still concerned about shortages, especially of English meat. There was only a very small amount available in the borough, because butchers were no longer permitted to buy fresh meat from Wickford Market, a right they had previously enjoyed. It was decided to contact the Divisional Food Commissioner, asking that the concession should once more be restored. Wartime restrictions were still causing real problems in the town.

Spanish Flu was also gaining momentum. By July it was reported to be reaching epidemic proportions in France  and by September  it was rapidly spreading in Britain. London's telegraph office was badly hit when 700 workers were absent through illness and the United States Federal Bureau of Health reported that more servicemen had died of influenza than of wounds suffered in battle. Many schools were closed because of the epidemic. Efforts to develop a vaccine had proved unsuccessful.

The use of gas in warfare caused long term problems. Private Alex Lamb, of the Black Watch, whose mother lived in Westcliff, was in hospital suffering from gas poisoning and shell shock and many others faced similar problems. Outwardly they may have appeared fit, but the damage was often as great as that caused by more obvious wounds.

While these worries persisted in Europe the Southend Petty Sessions had to deal with more mundane matters and in this case noise was the issue. Mrs Southerland was summoned for allowing a steam organ to be played at the Kursaal, causing aggravation to residents in nearby Southchurch Avenue. This happened in August, during the peak holiday season. Among those complaining, Mr Bond of Woodgrange Drive said that when he was at home in the evenings the music was a real nuisance. He worked at this time and needed to concentrate. He also stated that the machine played the same tunes all day long and was heard very plainly when the wind was from the south west. The defendant's husband pointed out that he had control of the machine and had been in the same line of work for twenty-seven years. Only once before had he been brought to court and that was when the organ was only twelve feet from the complainant's window. The machine could play any type of music and had a wide selection of tunes. Those serving in the trenches would probably have welcomed the sound of the organ rather than the constant noise of guns.

*A Great War aerodrome water tower.* (By kind permission of Stow Maries Great War Aerodrome)

There seemed to be a new feeling of optimism in the town. Estate Agents reported that they were nearly as busy as they had been before the war. Houses were described as 'letting like hot cakes' and good houses quickly found purchasers. The demand became so high that prices tended to rise rather than fall. In 1917 every street had several empty houses but by the summer of 1918 confidence had returned and it was very rare to see a notice offering a property to be let. The fear of air raids seemed to have been forgotten.

Excessive drinking was still a problem. In fact some churches opened unlicensed clubs to offer men companionship and games rooms to keep them away from public houses, especially at weekends. One such church was St Mary's, Prittlewell. A special room had been set aside, dating from 1904. At first darts was available and later a snooker/billiards table was added. Over the years the club flourished and grew. It now has five excellent snooker tables and is still welcoming members well over a hundred years later.

Thomas Connolly of Southend did not belong to such a group. He was a cutting machinist in an aeroplane factory and pleaded not guilty to a charge of being drunk in Alexander Street on a Saturday afternoon. PC Aspey said that he saw Mr Connolly sitting on a doorstep at 1.50 pm. His hat had fallen off and he was asleep. When woken he seemed incapable of taking care of himself, so the witness took him to the police station for his own safety. The defendant explained that he had been working all night and was very tired. He sat down to write some post cards and fell asleep. He insisted that he was more sleepy than drunk. He did not have a drink until 1pm and was taken to the police station before 2 o'clock. The court rejected his explanation and he was fined five shillings.

By October the Allies were making considerable advances in Europe, but the belief that the war would end quickly had disappeared. There was a feeling that this must simply be a brief respite and there were still long lists in the local papers of those killed or wounded.

Carrier pigeons were used by the government during the war and played a vital part as they transported messages. Unfortunately a number of these very useful birds had been shot by farmers. Prosecutions failed because it was said that a farmer had a lawful excuse for shooting pigeons on his own land. Much debate followed, with experts claiming that carrier pigeons were unlikely to eat corn from the fields where they alighted. They were probably searching for grubs or grit. Apart from that, any loss of grain would be negligible, but the loss of trained birds was a serious problem as they were needed for war purposes. An urgently amended regulation announced that it was an offence to shoot any carrier pigeon, except with the consent of the owner. Justices dealing with cases of shooting were asked to remember the urgent need to protect war birds.

The war might still be raging but development of the new Priory Park continued. A design for the main gates was published and an archaeological dig took place on the site of the former Lady Chapel. A librarian was searching for the tombstone of Thomas Richards, a major land owner in Prittlewell and Berkshire in the fifteenth century, He died in 1487 and his will stated that he wished to be buried before the altar of Our Lady of Pity in the manor church of Prittlewell. A coffin was discovered, which an archaeologist believed to be that of Thomas Richards. Only the lead shell remained with a cross and pole marks from where the coffin was carried. It faced due east and had not been moved from its original position. Mr Clay, the librarian, believed it was originally encased in a stone coffin, but the top stone had been taken away. It was thought the stone might have been used for paving in St Mary's churchyard, Prittlewell, at the top of the hill.

Archaeological digs seemed far removed from the war taking place in Europe but, by 7 November reports came in that the allies were slowly opening the way to Germany and not just from the west. An armistice with Austria-Hungary meant that, with Turkey and Bulgaria out of the war, Germany was effectively on her own. Within the German government there were two sides; one would rather perish than surrender, the other accepted the facts as they were and wished to make peace with the best grace possible. The peace party won; the terms for the signing of an armistice agreement were prepared.

As the final weekend came before the signatures were written on the momentous document there was a feeling of intense excitement and expectancy in the town. There was also a deep rooted fear that the Germans might still refuse to sign, thus extending the war for months to come.

When the abdication of Kaiser Wilhelm II was announced on 9 November in the window of the *Southend Standard* the news was greeted with jubilation. Surely peace must follow. 11 o'clock on Monday morning was the time when the armistice came into effect. Shortly after 10 o'clock there were rumours that hostilities had ceased. It was said that the Navy Office in Southend had received the information by wireless. Then the Queen Mary Royal Naval Hospital received a similar message, but most people wanted an official announcement. Even so, there was a rush by some to buy flags and red, white and blue favours. Then the siren on top of the sea front Gas Works, that had for so long been associated with air raids, was heard. Surely it could not herald another attack, but it kept sounding for the next seven minutes. What had been a harbinger of death now blasted out the news of peace.

By 14 November the town was bright with flags and bunting. Church services were held to give thanks for the peace. The Kursaal announced that a grand Victory Ball would be held on New Year's Eve with tickets costing one shilling. Life would soon return to normal - or would it? The war had changed so much and the lives of so many would never be quite the same again.

# CHAPTER 10

# Aftermath

With the signing of the Treaty of Versailles at the end of June 1919 the war was officially over; yet its after effects would echo down the years. Woman had played a very different and useful role during those terrible times. Some were only too eager to give up their jobs and return to home making, but there were many who had discovered a new found freedom and independence. It was something they were very reluctant to relinquish.

Some women now had the vote. To qualify they had to be over thirty and either they or their husband had to own property. The first woman to take her place in the House of Commons in 1919 was Nancy Astor. In fact the first female to be elected to a Parliamentary seat was Countess Constance de Markievicz in 1918. She was a Sinn Fein representative for the St Patrick's division of Belfast. She failed to take up her seat as she was in prison at the time, under suspicion for involvement with German conspirators during the war. Although she was eventually released, she failed to attend Parliament as her party was boycotting it at that time.

A General Election was held in December, 1918 and Rupert Guiness, Lord Elvedon, became Southend's new MP. He was a Conservative and had a majority of 8,150. This started a long link with members of the Guiness family, as they continued to represent the town until 1997

Many women had been widowed and some had a man returning home whose body or mind had been destroyed by the conflict. Children had been left without fathers. Life for them all would never be the same again.

*The Southend-on-Sea War Memorial.*

Official peace celebrations were organized throughout the town. In July 1919 there was a Naval Review, which included battleships, cruisers and submarines of the Atlantic Fleet. They were moored between Shoeburyness and Leigh and must have been an impressive sight. Later children from Hamstel Junior School were taken to Harwich to visit the captured U-Boat *Deutschland.*

Peace Day was held officially on 23 July 1919, when the battleships fired a twenty-one gun salute. Later there were fireworks and by night the whole fleet was illuminated. Peace Day was also a time for celebrations throughout the town. A carnival procession went from Southchurch Hall Park to the bandstand on the cliffs, there were yacht races and the school children of the town had their own special celebrations in the various parks. They were entertained by conjurers and clowns, had donkey rides and a Punch and Judy show. Afterwards every child received a bag of cakes and buns and later they were each given a longer lasting Peace Medal. In Priory Park there was a garden fete and another firework display.

As mentioned, during the war there had been temporary memorials erected to those already recorded as having died. They were known as 'War Shrines' and it was accepted that they would be replaced once the war had ended. An official War Memorial Committee was set up in January 1919, with the new Mayor, F.W. Senior, in the chair. Various ideas for suitable memorials were considered, including an extension to Victoria hospital, gardens at Prittlewell Square or cottages for ex-servicemen. Finally it was decided to place the main town memorial on top of the cliffs where a flagstaff had previously stood. Funds were raised from various sources, including the ever popular concerts. There was also a fishing festival held on the pier, which was highly successful. It was decided that any money left over after the erection of the memorial would be used to fund War Memorial Scholarships for those children with a parent whose name was included on the roll of honour.

Sir Edwin Lutyens was chosen to design the memorial and this was approved in 1921, the cost being £5,500. He was also responsible for the design of the Cenotaph in Whitehall and the massive Thriepval Memorial on the Somme. It was decided not to engrave a list of the fallen on the memorial, but to place the names on tablets to be mounted on the wall in the refectory of Prittlewell Priory. The finished War

*The memorial board in Priory Museum to Southend men who died in the Great War.* (By kind permission of Southend-on-Sea Central Museum)

*The inscription on the Southend War Memorial.*

Memorial was unveiled by the Lord Lieutenant on 27 November 1921 before specially invited guests and representatives from the many local organizations that had been involved in the war effort. The important guests included the Bishop of Chelmsford, E.C. Jones, the son of Robert A. Jones and Private Cannon. He had received the British Empire Medal for his efforts at the time of the 12 August air raid on Southend. Some of the towns and villages that formed the borough collected for their own memorials. In Eastwood alone £600 was raised.

In 1921 R.A. Jones made another generous gift to the town. This was the Victory Sports Ground. It was given to benefit the people of Southend, but very specially to commemorate all the sportsmen who gave their lives in the Great War. This great benefactor to the town died in 1925.

We often hear about the work done by horses and carrier pigeons in the Great War, but perhaps less is known about the role played by dogs. In 1917 Colonel Edwin Richardson set up a school for the training of dogs at Shoebury Barracks. They were at first recruited from Battersea Dogs Home and their work involved carrying messages across some of the most dangerous areas on the battlefields. The training school did its work well and the dogs showed great courage. Some were very badly injured, yet many still hauled themselves on to deliver their messages.

More than 7,000 dogs were trained at Shoebury Barracks and people often donated animals because they believed it would help to end the war. They were also trained to do rescue work, dragging wounded men back from No Man's Land. Later some survivors were retrained to act as companions and aids for those who had lost their sight in the war.

With the war was officially over Southend hoped to attract visitors back to the town. Lighting restrictions in coastal areas had been abandoned and sand bags and barbed wire removed from vulnerable areas. However, there was still a problem. German mines had been laid

*Southend bandstand with a military band playing.* (By kind permission of Southend-on-Sea Central Museum)

in local waters and these were swept ashore for some years after the conflict ended. Constant vigilance was needed, especially at low tide, when unwanted hazards could be deposited on the mud flats. Children were only too keen to pick up souvenirs from the war and the results could be disastrous.

Men who had served in the armed services wanted to be home as soon as possible, but this was not an option for everyone. Britain still had commitments in Germany, Russia and the garrisons of the Empire. Those like miners, whose specialist skills were needed at home, were the first to be demobbed. Then came those who had volunteered early, but conscripts and 18-year-olds were left until last. Regular soldiers remained until their period of service was completed.

*James George Winn, aged 17, of West Road, Westcliff.* (With thanks to Bill and Doreen Sawford)

Demobilization took time. Before being able to leave his unit, each man had to face a medical examination. After this he received Army Form Z22. This allowed him to claim for any disability caused by his military service. Then he needed the Plain Clothes Form, Z44 and he also needed a Certificate of Employment, which showed what his role had been in the forces. This was Z18. Next there was a Dispersal Certificate, recording not only personal and military information but also the state of his equipment. After this time, if anything was lost or damaged, the cost of replacement would be deducted from his pay. Next he would go to a transit camp. This would be near the coast, prior to sailing home.

Once back on home soil there would be a journey to a Dispersal Centre. Here the men waited in tents, huts or barracks. A Protection Certificate was issued to each man so that he could receive medical attention, if needed, during his final leave. He was also given a railway ticket or warrant to his nearest home station. By the end of 1919 nearly all those who were not professional soldiers were home once more.

In the trenches men had lived together in close proximity. This led to infections spreading quickly. Unfortunately Spanish Flu was still active and some of those returning home carried the virus to their families. The epidemic remained a major health problem.

The hotels and other buildings that had been used as hospitals during the war now returned to their former roles, including was Queen Mary's Royal Naval Hospital, which had done such sterling work throughout the conflict. Once again it reverted to its old name, the Palace Hotel.

As the troops returned, not everyone was able to find employment. The town council decided to build a market in York Road. This created some work and food and other necessities became available at reduced prices.

By the end of the war cinemas were becoming ever more important. In Southend several new ones opened. One of these was The Star in West Street, next door to the Blue Boar Public house. At that time all the films were silent and in black and white. In spite of a recent refurbishment the Empire Theatre closed its doors for the last time in 1919, but later re-opened as the Rivoli cinema.

Another park also opened in the same year, this time at Belfairs. It was bought by the council for £20,000 and its eighteen-hole golf course became extremely popular. In Southchurch Park, cricket was again being played. Early in the war, when soldiers were drilling in the park, they were firmly told that the wicket area must not be used. That meant it was still in reasonable condition and so could be the venue for a match against the Australian Imperial Force. The visitors won by 309 runs. Football, too, continued to be played. Southend United originally played at Roots Hall, but in 1919 the team moved to the Kursaal, where the pitch was overlooked by the well known water chute. The old ground fell into disuse. It was many years later that Roots Hall once again became the popular venue for home matches.

Southend-on-Sea now settled into the post war era. It regained its status as a popular seaside town. The world had changed and so had the town.  The War to End all Wars was over. As the 1920s dawned there was a new belief in the future and a general feeling of optimism and hope.

# Bibliography

*Zepplins over Southend* by Ken Crowe (Southend Museums, 2008)
*Chronicle of the 20th Century* (Longmans, 1988)
*Southend Standard* 1914-1918
*Echo News* article by Tom King (3 January 2014
*The Last Great War* by Adrian Gregory (CUP, 2008)
*Front Line Essex* by Michael Foley (Sutton Publishing, 2005)
*More Front-Line Essex* by Michael Foley (The History Press, 2008)
*The Great War* by John D. Clare (Hodder & Stoughton, 2004)
*The Story of Southend Pier* by E.W. Shepherd (Egon Publishers Ltd, 1979)
*Essex Airmen 1910-1918* by John Barfoot (Tempus Publishing, 2006)
*Sagittarius Rising* by Cecil Lewis (Frontline Books, Pen & Sword Books)
*The Impact of Catastrophe* by Paul Rusiecki (Essex Record Office)

# Index

Agnes, Carter, 73–4
Agriculture, 53, 62, 67, 74, 84, 89
Armistice, 97

Battle of Jutland, 47
Battle of the Somme, 51, 53, 59
Beeton Lieutenant A.C., 33–4, 45
British Expeditionary Force, 12, 17
Burrows, H.H., 32–3

Cobweb Corner, 24, 26, 53, 72
Conscription, 40, 52
Corri Family, 92

Defence of the Realm Act, 11, 88
Demobilization, 104
Derby Scheme, 36, 38–40, 68

Essex Regiment, 13, 16, 33–4, 40

Flechettes, 16
Florence Gowers, 74
Food Control Committee, 77, 79–80, 94

Francis, Alderman Joseph (Mayor), 36, 39, 82
Gas Poisoning, 28, 94

Hance, Arthur, 25, 75
Heavy Bombers, 47, 49, 66, 68, 72, 74
Holthof, Chaplin J., 26
Home Fleet, 9

Jones, R.A., 42, 86–7, 102

Kitchener, Lord, 47
Kursaal, 10, 43, 94, 97, 105

Lewis, Cecil, 49
Lowen, D.J., 37–8
Lutyens, Sir Edwin, 100

Manning Horace, 40–1
Massie, Major J.A., 16
Medals, 54, 86–7, 93
Mediterranean Expeditionary Force, 37
Military Deferment, 52, 60–1, 76–7, 83
    Exemption, 45–7, 85
Military Service Act, 45, 68, 86

Pier, 11-12, 36, 100
  civilian use, 7–8, 21–2, 54–5,
    84
Priory Park, 34, 83, 86–7, 96,
  100
Prison Ships, 11–12, 22
Prisoners of War, 90–1

Queen Mary's Royal Naval
  Hospital, 13–14, 26, 31, 58,
  76, 97, 105
  fund raising, 19, 69, 78, 92

Rochford Aerodrome, 10, 47–9,
  56, 72, 86
Royal Air Force, 86
Royal Flying Corps, 16, 49
Royal Visits, 7, 29–30, 43, 69

Scouting, 35–6
Shoeburyness, 10, 16, 24, 26,
  43–4, 70, 100, 103
  barracks and garrison, 10, 16,
    26, 103
Southend Battalion of the
  National Guard, 34

Southend Standard, 9, 15, 25, 42,
  83–4,
  overseas reports, 29, 37, 45,
    97
Spanish Flu, 88, 94, 105
Submarine Attacks, 53, 62, 64,
  66–7, 92

Tolhurst, Alfred, 13
Toronto Star, 40

Volunteer Training Corps, 82
Volunteer Watch, 34

War Loans, 31
War Memorials, 34, 70, 99–102
War Pensions Committee, 70
Westborough School, 23, 81

Zeppelins, 15, 19, 31–2, 43–4,
  55–6, 68, 78
  Southend-on-Sea attacks, 21–
    4, 26, 34, 47–9
  Count Ferdinand von Zeppelin,
    21, 66